Coast 2 Coast Mentoring LLC.

Coast 2 Coast Mentoring LLC.

THE HEALTHCARE RECRUITING TRAINING MANUAL OF THE PRESENT & FUTURE

Created by

Noah Neumiller

ISBN: 9798654987099 (paperback)

TABLE OF CONTENTS

CHAPTER 1

Introduction: Coast 2 Coast Mentoring LLC.

Being a young entrepreneur in a very competitive industry, over the past seventeen years I have had many successes that did not prepare me for the inevitable realization that every day is not a glorious day, simply because after experiencing a high volume of success as I did, you have to know how to manage it. That is where I dealt with the frustrations that have ultimately resulted in a complete change in my attitude and understanding of this very complex industry, leaving me with moments of reflection through my trials and tribulations that have inspired me to help inexperienced yet motivated prospective recruiters strive for success and opportunity, providing the tools to create a maintainable revenue stream while keeping a unrestrictive schedule all from the comforts of home.

I have worked all areas of the healthcare staffing industry from Jr. Recruiter to Director of Lead Healthstaff, possessing years of one on one experience training recruiters, working alongside pioneers of the in the industry and even innovating the recruiting cycle with team members. I am passionate about helping others exceed pinnacles and expectations both personally and for the agency they are employed by.

In order to produce results and solve problems, you must possess the ability to envision the bigger picture to pave the path to success while understanding the ins and outs of the industry in great detail. I have seen firsthand and been on the receiving end of endless financial opportunities for both recruiters and owners alike. My goal is for you to grow as a recruiter from my personal experience which I believe will be beneficial as you journey through this very competitive yet fruitful industry.

Establishing Company Creditably/ Self-Rapport

Establish who your company is. You want to have a rebuttal for questions like who is your healthcare company? What do they represent? What services do they perform? You want to have these questions answered when speaking to travelers or healthcare clients and what you would you tell them.

Talking about yourself or your company is your occasion to make genuine and enlighten connection with candidate. You always want to make sure you are being authentic. Too many healthcare recruiters fall into being someone they are not. It's vital to know what your company caters and why they do so. When speaking be smooth and polished with a positive/assuring tone.

What is key strength talking points about your company? For example, I would say my company is Joint Commission Certified as well as hold golden seal of approval. What are your duties with companies? Example, I would state to increase production 25% and build a better foundation with company clients. What separate's you versus the next recruiter? For example, I would state I have 18 years+ straight healthcare recruiting experience and have shattered every production record with any company I worked with and have the production reports to verify. What values and assets do you hold that's important to the future of your company? Example, I would rebuttal that I continue to strive for success which production numbers verify and willing to go above and beyond helping others without being asked.

You want to also know answers to questions like what is your company's organizational structure? For example, know who your Owner, Vice president, HR, Supervisor, Manager etc. is and a little about each of them. Who does what & why? Example know what role each individual play within your organization and how it's vital to company's success. Your role is to establish rapport with qualified candidates for clients then send to review to seal an offer.

Another key is to establish what is the vision of your company? For example, my company I work for Lead Healthstaff was founded with the mission of providing the highest quality nursing and allied professionals to healthcare facilities by utilizing advanced recruitment systems and providing unparalleled customer service. How long has your company been established? Example, I would say Lead Healthstaff has been operating since 2010. Over 10+ years. What is the vision and goals or your company? For example, I would state, we recognize the challenges in today's health care staffing industry. New choices, new opportunities and new standards, brought on by high-tech medicine, rigid industry accreditation and rapidly escalating costs, present a challenging and engaging operating environment while creating a greater demand for experienced healthcare professionals. This environment demands leadership and Lead Healthstaff is uniquely positioned and willing to help both healthcare facilities and healthcare professionals make the right choices for the times ahead. Our experienced team of senior managers and recruiters possess a vast knowledge of the industry and prides themselves on one-on-one personal service, which in turn translates into top-level satisfaction ratings from our clients and candidates. Lead Healthstaff has received certification from the Joint Commission (JCAHO) and is an active member of the National Association of Travel Healthcare Organizations (NATHO).

Your mission and vision should be backed by every action and decision. Be consistent with your vision and mission. Your personal or company vision and mission form the foundation for how you operate business. They serve as a outline for your decisions. They keep them aligned with your pinnacles or goals. Eventually this is why others should care you are in business and why they would want you to represent and do business with you.

Healthcare Industry Overview – Coast 2 Coast Mentoring LLC.

Why Do Hospitals Hire Travelers?

Hiring traveling nurses rather than permanent nurses eliminates the need to pay for benefits such as health insurance, retirement and paid days off. As well as reduces recruiting, training overtime and payroll costs.

Nurses make up the largest profession in the United States at estimated over 3 million. Despite those numbers the healthcare industry is facing insufficiency of grand proportions.

One third of the current country's nursing with be retiring within the upcoming decade being they are fifty years of age or plus.

Our baby boomer generation is aging. The generation is most often defined as individuals born between 1946 and 1964, during the post-World War two baby boom. That's roughly twenty percent. When doing the numbers, one in five Americans will be fifty-five plus (senior citizens.) Remarkable rise in chronic diseases and the demand for healthcare/medical attention. American sixty years of age and plus are expected to rise from over forty million back in 2010 to seventy-three million within a decade. Ninety percent of those have a chronic condition with seventy percent have multiple health issues. Making them three times more likely to visit a hospital each year. Elderly have a longer average stay versus any other age group.

Another great reason is due to the rising number of Americans insured because of the Affordable Care Act (ACA), which is forecasted to supply twenty-five million previously uninsured Americans with healthcare coverage within the year 2020. Since Affordable Care Act, reimbursement payments are being aligned with quality metrics, customer satisfaction as well as lower readmission rates. Hospitals have to hire additional staff to produce a better patient-care domain and keep hospital staff from experiencing exhaustion. Many are pushing for lower patient ratios and stronger support to balance fatigue.

Crucial element is nursing schools do not have the capacity let alone proven to be able to maintain with the demand and have little capacity for the amount of nursing students that they are able to get enrolled each school year. Limitations of the American healthcare educational system, for instance when a student nurse completes graduation, they cannot just get employed. Hospitals have requirements looking to hire RN's with hands-on acute care hospital setting experience anywhere from a minimal of one to two years. Due to the fact that hospitals aren't well equipped to educate and have the proper time to train new nurses.

Various hospitals, being a less desired locations, have a hard time employing or keeping nurses on staff. Many reasons to why hospitals desire the need to fill gaps in staff. Some female nurses are on maternity leaves, or taking family and medical leave, or surgical leaves.

The healthcare travel nursing was reported to have been created in the 1970's and is projected to grow for decades to come. Unfortunately, people will always have some sort of health concerns, needing hospital attention. The healthcare industry is over a two-billion-dollar industry. Over eleven billion if you include allied health and per diem/locum tenens.

Healthcare Industry Influencers & Healthcare Market Share – Coast 2 Coast Mentoring LLC.

Healthcare industry revenues are exceeding pinnacles in all facets. Competition amongst agencies to provide qualified professionals molding clients criteria's ferocious. VMS/MSP vendor management systems control over sixty-five percent of the healthcare staffing industry. Mergers and investments have played a great role impacting healthcare industry market share. Many corporate healthcare companies have acquired and positioned smaller companies under their protection, which contributes to calculated growth.

Several executive professional organizations serve the healthcare staffing industry in a vital way, primarily the Joint Commission and The National Association of Travel Healthcare Organizations.

- The Joint Commission is a well-known certification program that is a global driver of quality improvement and patient safety in health care. Through leading practices, unmatched knowledge and expertise, and rigorous standards, they help organizations across the continuum of care lead the way to zero harm. They are considered the guidelines for quality among healthcare companies. It's a way to gauge the qualification and proficiency practices for your company. Once certified with the Joint Commission they will drop in once every two years to survey practices and make sure companies are following their requirements.

– NATHO – The National Association of Travel Healthcare Organizations. Founded in 2008 to promote ethical business practices in the travel healthcare industry, setting the gold standard for conduct that is aligned among member agencies on behalf of travel healthcare candidates and clients. Members are held to a strict code of ethics that was developed specifically for the Travel Healthcare industry.

Key influencers maintain a strong hold through social media such as Facebook groups, LinkedIn groups, Gypsy Nurse and Blue Pipes to name a few. This will continue for decades to come.

Healthcare Contracting Process – Coast 2 Coast Mentoring LLC.

When staffing has a shortage at a hospital, they contract with agencies to fill those needs. Hospitals are contracted with multiple agencies even during low census.

When a hospital releases/opens a job order, hospital staffing team contacts agencies and provides full details and any requirements they deem ample to fill that job order. Agencies transmit those requirements to internal staff. Recruiters then seek qualified candidates molding client's requirements to seal an offer versus another recruiter. Traditionally, once the recruitment team identifies qualified candidates, the account manager sends the candidate submission packet profile to be reviewed. If manager of unit is interested, you will either receive an interview and sometimes an offer. Meaning based on your profile they possibly will grant your company an offer based on how strong your profile is.

Once the hospital has interviewed, if they deem, you're a fit, the hospital will send an offer via email or notified by phone to your company. Next step, the recruiter will communicate to nurse and confirm in writing the nurse accepts offer agreed upon. The recruiter sends a contract to nurse for signature to seal in writing. Once contract is signed by nurse, account manager sends a contract to hospital confirming the traveler's conformation.

Compliance and agency onboarding are next step once contract signed by traveler. Compliance team and recruiters work simultaneously to secure all compliance paperwork requirements in order to be cleared for traveler to start assignment on start date agreed upon on signed contract.

Educate Yourself on Your Competitors – Coast 2 Coast Mentoring LLC.

To compete in today's healthcare recruiting market price is a huge factor, but not determining factor. Transparency is the best asset any recruiter can adopt. The best healthcare recruiters do. Candidates choose recruiters who best mold their needs and who provides the most value. It's nothing personal.

How you cater and attention to detail you display differentiates you from your competition creating a moment of magic customer service experience. Educating and understanding your competitions weaknesses are key.

For recruiters, most agencies offer these standard benefits below to their healthcare candidates:

- Medical, dental, vision coverage
- 401k plan/Retirement
- Travel Reimbursement
- Referral Bonus
- Joint Commission Certification
- Car rental
- Flight booking
- Certification/License reimbursement
- 24/7 accessibility
- Tax advantage
- Professional liability insurance
- Housing/Meals Untaxed Stipends

Extra Perks Some Agencies Aide In:

- Guaranteed Hours
- Paid time off (PTO)
- Sick Pay
- Company support staff after hours
- Disability insurance
- Vendor Management Service (VMS) / Managed Service Provider (MSP) exclusive contracts
- License application service and support
- Corporate discounts for various product/services
- Class-finding services for travelers needed updates for expired/expiring certifications

- License application assistance
- Loyalty programs
- Resume services
- Free CEU's – continuing education online services
- Registry/Per Diem contracts
- Life insurance

CHAPTER 2

Industry Overview – Coast 2 Coast Mentoring LLC.

Healthcare Nursing Introduction – Coast 2 Coast Mentoring LLC.

Nurses play a vital role in our healthcare system, by helping patients learn how to make healthy choices at the bedside, understand their doctor's diagnosis, and how to manage symptoms. They then arm patients with the best information at discharge, so they understand what to do once they get home. Over the years, nurses have helped improve access to care. Blazes new paths in telehealth, informatics, technology development, and genomics. Nurses work to reduce medical errors and improve patient safety. Promote wellness and expand preventive care. Engage in research with practical equipment and impact. Not to mention advocation for patients. American Nursing Association states nurses are responsible for the following standards and guidelines of healthcare practice.

- – Planning
- – Assessment
- – Coordination of care
- – Nursing diagnosis

- Consultation
- Implementation
- Evaluation
- Prescriptive authority and treatment
- Health teaching and health wellness

Nurses are creative and some innovators to moving the healthcare industry forward for decades. Six healthcare innovations you may not know were created by nurses.

1. 1850s: Florence Nightingale – Hygiene Protocols and Patient Services
2. 1940s: Bessie Blount Griffin – Feeding Tube for Paralyzed Veterans
3. 1950s: Sister Jean Ward – Neonatal Phototherapy
4. 1960s: Anita Dorr – Crash Cart
5. 2000s: Teri Barton-Salina and Gail Barton-Hay – Color-coded IV Lines
6. 2010s: Neomi Bennett – Neo-slip®

In this chapter, if you are unfamiliar with certain healthcare terms for unit departments and procedures, please consult the glossary towards the end of the manual for definitions.

Formulating Pitch: Tone, Delivery, Message

When it comes to your pitch, be yourself. Let your personality come through and don't sound like a robot. Change things up and make sure that you are using enthusiasm in your tone and voice inflection/intonation.

What does that even mean?

It's not what you say or how you say it, but how the person hears it.

You can lead a horse to water, but you can't make him drink. However, you can make him thirsty!

"Yes, But, Because, Their Name, If, help and Thanks," are some magic words that can be persuasive when trying to sell a candidate on a location, job, or pay.

The use of filler words can make you sound like you are not confident about the subject matter. Common filler words are, "um, uh, er, ah, like, okay, right, and you know."

Try to practice speaking without using these.

Example Scripts:

Hello Candidate,
this is recruiter from _____. I came across your resume on (Monster, Career Builder, Zip, Indeed, Beyond). We are trying to fill some RN positions in your area and your resume molds what we are looking for. Our pay packages are amongst the top in the industry. When you have a minute please give me a call at _____, ext. _____. Again, my name is recruiter with _____, I look forward to speaking with you.

Hello _____,
This is _____ with _____. I wanted to call you because I have several hospitals looking for a great RN like yourself. Your resume looks fantastic and I could really use your assistance filling one of these spots, not to mention it's great paying with a three thousand completion bonus. Please give me a call at _____ ext. _____. Thank you and I look forward to hearing from you.

Hi ___,

Hope you're having a blessed day. Crisis rates developed and will not last! I'm looking for CNAs/LPNs who match your experience to complete travel contracts in _____. If you or someone you know is interested, please contact me today as the facility's ready to start conducting interviews soon. You can reach me at _____ x _____. Thanks so much!

Creating and Leaving Voicemails: Coast 2 Coast Mentoring LLC.

This is _____ with _____. I'm reaching out to you to see if you are available or just open to hearing about new nursing positions? I staff for several of the top hospitals here in the nation and when I was going through my database this morning, I noticed your skills match up with a lot of these open RN positions. So, when you get some time, if you are available, if you're looking to make more money or just want a better work life balance, feel free to reach back out to me. My number is…...Thank you.

Hi this is _____ I'm a recruiter with ____, I'm reaching out to you today in regard to your resume as I was very impressed, looks like you would be a great match for some of our assignments I have available. When you get a moment please give me a call at _____ ext. _____ Thank you. Have a great day!

Good Morning! This is _____ with _____. I wanted to reach out and see if you might be looking for a new contract in the next couple of months. I have several hospitals looking for great nurses and they are looking to interview today. Please give me a call when you have a minute.

Hey___! This is _____ with _____I saw you might be looking for some ICU jobs in California. I have 3-5 hospitals that need help right now. If you are still looking please let me know. I would love to help.

Hey___! I wanted to check in and see how your current assignment is going. I have a few nurses looking to go to the area. Have a wonderful day!

"Hi Lisa, my name is _____ and I'm with _____ . I popped across some of your information and your old resume here and noticed that I have some high paying travelling assignments in the Hawaii area that I think would be perfect for you. Give me a call back at _____ ext. _____. Again, it's ___ with _____. Talk to you soon!"

"Hi Devin, my name is _____ and I am calling from _____! Wanted to check in on you to see what you've been up to in the nursing world and let you know that I am looking to fill a few travel contracts in Arizona. Have a few hospitals looking for some help here over the next 3-6 months. If you are interested and available, give me a call at _____ ex _____. Thanks, Devin – I will talk with you soon!"

Healthcare Hospital Requirements List – Coast 2 Coast Mentoring LLC.

Minimum Requirements

Most facilities require a certain level of hands-on experience to become a travel nurse. Years of experience can range but you will need at least one-year experience as an RN within an acute care hospital setting to become a travel nurse. Joint Commission certification program helps to ensure that the superior quality of traveling healthcare candidates is being matched to client hospitals. It is crucial healthcare candidates must be punctual, flexible, adaptable, able to work independently and help co-workers without being asked. Hospitals generally are understaffed and do not have time to train after orientation. Travelers are excepted to pretty much hit the ground running. Candidates need to able to solve problems independently with minimal supervision. Common healthcare hospital requirements are:

- Clean Background – no actions or felonies against license. Misdemeanors may eliminate a potential candidate from receiving an offer depending on hospitals policies.
- Minimum recent one-year acute care hospital setting experience.
- Two references from a charge, managers or supervisors within the last year.
- Active unit certifications and licensure through the American Heart Association (AHA).

Healthcare Nursing Degrees – Coast 2 Coast Mentoring LLC.

Healthcare Nursing Degrees

To obtain a license to become a registered nurse (RN) you must complete the steps below:

1. Take college prep classes in high school

- In addition to a U.S. high school education or the equivalent as described in Section 1412 of the Board›s regulations to become a registered nurse (RN), you should take the following classes in high school and you will have a head start on your nursing class prerequisites at college:
  - English – 4 years

- › Math – 3-4 years (including algebra and geometry)
- › Science – 2-4 years (including biology and chemistry; physics and computer science are recommended)
- › Social Studies – 3-4 years
- › Foreign Language – 2 years
- Check out nursing prerequisites at colleges you are considering.
- Individual nursing schools vary in their nursing course prerequisites. Talk to your high school guidance counselor and check out the websites of the California nursing schools you are considering.

2. Choose the type of nursing school you want to attend

In California, there are three types of pre-licensure nursing programs, and two alternative routes to become a registered nurse:

- **Associate Degree in Nursing (ADN)**
  Takes 2-3 years. Offered at many community colleges. Prepares you to provide registered nursing care in numerous settings.

- **Bachelor of Science in Nursing (BSN)**
  Takes 4 years. Also referred to as Baccalaureate degree. Offered at many California State Universities and some private colleges. Prepares you to provide registered nursing care in numerous settings and to move to administrative and leadership positions.

- **Entry Level Master's Program in Nursing (ELM)**
  Designed for adults who have a baccalaureate degree in another field and wish to become registered nurses. Takes 1-2 years

depending on how many nursing course prerequisites you have already completed. Graduate receives a master's degree.

- **LVN 30 Unit Option**
  Designed as a career ladder for California Licensed Vocational Nurses wishing to become registered nurses. Takes approximately 18-24 months. No degree is granted upon completion. Most other states do not recognize California's LVN 30 Unit Option and will not issue RN licenses to these LVNs. Some LVNs prefer to complete an ADN program in order to obtain a degree and to have the flexibility to get an RN license in other states. Most ADN programs will give LVNs credit for some of the coursework they completed to become an LVN.

- **Military Corpsmen**
  California law permits military corpsmen to take the national exam for RN licensure if they have completed RN level education and clinical experience.

3. Select a college and apply for admission

- Visit the websites and campuses of the colleges in the geographic areas of interest to you. You can choose from over 140 California nursing schools.
- Find out which entry exams are required at the colleges you are considering.
- Apply at more than one college to give yourself options. Many colleges have limited space for nursing students.

4. Apply for financial aid

Opportunities abound for scholarships, loans, and loan forgiveness programs. Please visit the Financial Aid Information section of our website for more information.

5. Obtain an RN license

To practice as an RN in California, you must be licensed by the California Board of Registered Nursing (BRN). You must meet educational requirements, pass a criminal background check, and pass the national licensing examination. To apply for licensure:

- <u>Apply online</u> or obtain an application packet and detailed instructions from the <u>BRN website.</u>
- Send your application to the BRN at least 6-8 weeks before graduation.
- Have your school send your transcripts to the BRN.
- Complete a <u>fingerprint background check.</u>
- Take and pass the National Council Licensing Examination (NCLEX). The exam is computerized and given continuously 6 days a week. (New graduates are advised to take the exam soon after graduation because research has shown that there is a higher success rate for early test takers compared with those who wait several months.)
- Apply for an Interim Permit if you wish to work in a supervised nursing capacity while awaiting the results of your examination.

**** Key Question to Ask

Does your agency offer education incentives such as an RN-to-BSN service? If so, what are the details?

Hospitals breakdown the field into particular units to provide a wide span of service as well as deliver top patient care.

Specialty:

- ER (Emergency Room)
- ICU (Intensive Care Unit)
- OR (Operating Room)
- OR Tech
- PACU (Post Anesthesia Care Unit)
- LD (Labor and Delivery)
- NICU (Neonatal Intensive Care Unit)
- PICU (Pediatric Intensive Care Unit)
- Cath Lab (Cardiac Catheterization Lab)

Non-Specialty:

- Med Surg (Medical/Surgical)
- Tele (Telemetry)
- Peds (Pediatrics)
- Psych (Behavioral Health)
- Onc (Oncology)

Extra Non-Specialty Nursing Areas:

- LTC/LTAC (Long-Term Care/Long-Term Acute Care) Hospice
- Dialysis

- Rehabilitation
- LPN (Licensed Practical Nurse)
- CNA (Certified Nursing Assistant)
- HH (Home Health)

Allied Health Areas:

- Rad (Radiology—X-ray, CT, MRI, Mammo, Ultrasound, Echo, Vascular) PT/PTA (Physical Therapist/Physical Therapist Assistant)
- OT (Occupational Therapist)
- RT (Respiratory Therapist)
- MT/MLT (Medical Technologist/Medical Laboratory Technician) Radiation Therapist/Dosimetrist
- Phlebotomist

Healthcare Specialty Unit Areas: Coast 2 Coast Mentoring LLC.

Unit Specialty Areas:

INTENSIVE CARE UNIT/CRITICAL CARE UNIT: Intensive care refers to the specialized treatment given to patients who are acutely unwell and require critical medical care. An intensive care (ICU) provides the critical care and life support for acutely ill and injured patients.

CERTIFICATIONS: ACLS, BLS, NIHSS
(REQUIREMENTS MAY VARY BASED ON FACILITY PREFERENCE)
FEATURES: Works with vented patients; high-acuity; critical patients; EKG—interpretation of cardiac rhythms

NURSE-TO-PATIENT RATIO: 1:1–2

Subdivisions: CVICU, MICU, SICU, Burn ICU, Neuro ICU

FLOATING: Not unless specified, but possibly to step down or ER holding units

EXAMPLES OF PATIENTS CARED FOR:

- Transfer from ER Requiring Close Monitoring
- Life-Threatening Illness/Injury
- Patients from Inpatient
- Units Who Deteriorate Rapidly
- Medical
- Post-Surgical
- Trauma
- Burn
- Cardiac

Questions to ask an ICU RN: What is the interpretation of CVP and PA pressure waveform with respiratory variation? Which tools should the nurse use to assess delirium in a critically ill patient? What is your skill sets with ART lines, LVAD, CVP, CRRT, IABP, EMCO and sheath removal? Are you comfortable floating? If so, what units have you floated to? Do you have NIHSS or CCRN certifications.

EMERGENCY ROOM UNIT: ER nurses treat patients who are suffering from trauma, injury or severe medical conditions and require urgent treatment. Since these specialists work in crisis situations, they must be able to quickly identify the best way to stabilize patients and minimize pain.

CERTIFICATIONS: TNCC, PALS, ACLS, BLS and possibly ENPC (REQUIREMENTS MAY VARY BASED ON FACILITY PREFERENCE)
FEATURES: Works closely with ER physicians; fast-paced; unpredictable; diverse patient population
NURSE-TO-PATIENT RATIO: 1:3–5
Subdivisions: Trauma, ER Holding
FLOATING: Not unless specified, for ER typically not

EXAMPLES OF PATIENTS CARED FOR:

- Trauma
- Fractures
- Auto Accidents
- Farming/Industrial Accidents / Chest Pain
- Heart Attack
- Stroke
- Acute Exacerbations
- COPD
- Asthma
- Mental Illness
- Withdrawal
- Overdose

Questions to ask an ER RN: What are the 3 types of trauma? Do you hold ENPC certification? What trauma level or levels do you have acute care hospital setting experience in? Are you Peds ER? Or Adult ER?

OPERATING ROOM UNIT: Operating room nursing is a specialized field in which nurses provide quality care to patients before, during and after surgery. An operating room nurse must have the same knowledge and skills as other registered nurses, but certain skills are even more invaluable during surgical procedures.

CERTIFICATIONS: BLS
(REQUIREMENTS MAY VARY BASED ON FACILITY PREFERENCE)
FEATURES: Circulating—remain in unsterile field; monitor and document during procedure
Scrubbing—in sterile field; aid surgeons by handing them equipment like sponges and other instruments
NURSE-TO-PATIENT RATIO: 1:1
Subdivisions: Scrub, Circ, First Assist (RNFA), CVOR
FLOATING: Not unless specified, for OR typically not

EXAMPLES OF PATIENTS CARED FOR:

- Thoracic
- Orthopedic
- General
- Neuro/Spine
- Endoscopy
- GU; Urology
- Cardiovascular
- Oral ENT
- Plastics (Reconstructive/Cosmetic)
- Transplant
- GYN
- Ophthalmology ENT
- Podiatry

Questions to ask an OR RN: What are four 4 basic principles of surgical nursing that you as the EN need to practice? Are you okay with being on-call? Do you Scrub, Circulate or both? Do you prefer eight-hour shifts, ten-hour shifts or twelve-hour shifts?

OPERATING ROOM TECH: Surgical technicians, also known surgical technologists or operating room technicians, prepare operating rooms, set up equipment and surgical tools, and assist doctors and nurses during surgeries as instructed. Surgical techs have differing responsibilities.

CERTIFICATIONS: BLS & CST
(REQUIREMENTS MAY VARY BASED ON FACILITY PREFERENCE)
FEATURES: Prepare and transport patients, set up equipment, surgical instruments, and other supplies in the operating room, assist surgeons with scrubbing and dressing
NURSE-TO-PATIENT RATIO: 1:1
Subdivisions: None
FLOATING: Not unless specified, for ER typically not

EXAMPLES OF PATIENTS CARED FOR:

- Thoracic
- Orthopedic
- General
- Neuro/Spine
- Endoscopy
- GU; Urology
- Cardiovascular

- Oral ENT
- Plastics (Reconstructive/Cosmetic)
- Transplant
- GYN
- Ophthalmology ENT
- Podiatry

Questions to ask an OR Tech: Which areas in the OR do you specialize in? Are you certified as a surgical tech? Have you worked in large or small OR rooms? Are you okay with call?

POST ANESTHESIA CARE UNIT: A post-anesthesia care unit (PACU) nurse cares for patients who have gone under anesthesia. They are responsible for observing and treating a patient post-operation and making sure that they safely awake from anesthesia.

CERTIFICATIONS: BLS & ACLS
(REQUIREMENTS MAY VARY BASED ON FACILITY PREFERENCE)
FEATURES: Recover surgical patients after procedure; manage pain for patients after surgery; may provide pre-op care of patient
NURSE-TO-PATIENT RATIO: 1:1–2
Subdivisions: None
FLOATING: Not unless specified, for PACU typically not

EXAMPLES OF PATIENTS CARED FOR:

- Adult
- Pediatric

- Orthopedic
- Cardiac
- GU
- Endoscopy
- Ophthalmology
- Neuro Trauma
- Transplant

Questions to ask an PACU RN: What Aldrete score must the patient have in Phase I recovery in order to be transferred to Phase II recovery? What are the criteria for discharge from the PACU? How often are vitals taken in PACU? Do you have the skill set to work pre and post op or both? Do you have acute care experience with chest tubes and extubating patients? Are you comfortable with call? Do you deal with Adults or Peds patients?

LABOR AND DELIVERY UNIT: Labor and delivery nurses administer medications, including epidurals, and assist physicians or midwives with the actual delivery. Following the birth, their care extends to the newborn and mother's needs. Labor and delivery nurses also help new mother-baby pairs with the baby's first breastfeeding.

CERTIFICATIONS: BLS, ACLS, NRP & AWHONN
(REQUIREMENTS MAY VARY BASED ON FACILITY PREFERENCE)
FEATURES: Monitor, assess, and assist with labor; some L&D nurses circulate C-sections
NURSE-TO-PATIENT RATIO: 1:1–2
Subdivisions: High Risk, Mother/Baby, Postpartum, Nursery, OB/GYN

FLOATING: Not unless specified, sometimes to post-partum or mother/baby

EXAMPLES OF PATIENTS CARED FOR:

- Pre-Labor
- Intra-Labor
- Post-Labor
- Newborn Infant
- High-Risk

Questions to ask an L&D RN: How dilated do you have to be before C section? Do you have high risk labor and delivery experience within an acute care hospital setting? Have you floated to Post-partum? What type of experience circulating during C-sections do you have?

NEONATAL INTENSIVE CARE UNIT: A neonatal nurse is a Registered Nurse (RN) that works in a Neonatal Intensive Care Unit (NICU) and assesses, monitors, and cares for medically fragile newborns. In addition to caring for premature newborns, NICU nurses may care for medically complex infants up to one year of age in some facilities.

CERTIFICATIONS: BLS, ACLS, NRP & AWHONN
(REQUIREMENTS MAY VARY BASED ON FACILITY PREFERENCE)
FEATURES: Works with neonatal patients; high acuity; critical patients; vents and cardiac monitoring
NURSE-TO-PATIENT RATIO: 1:1–2
Subdivisions: Level I-IV
FLOATING: Not unless specified, not for NICU unit

EXAMPLES OF PATIENTS CARED FOR:

- Prematurity
- Sepsis
- Hydrocephalus
- ECMO
- Congenital Viral Infections
- Meconium Aspiration
- Congenital Heart Disease
- Gastroschisis
- Hypoxic-Ischemic Encephalopathy
- Pneumothorax
- Hypoglycemia
- Choanal Atresia

Questions to ask an NICU RN: Do you have any experience floating PICU? What NICU Level or levels do you have acute experience in?

PEDIATRIC INTENSIVE CARE UNIT: No one ever said that a nursing career was easy on the mind, body, or soul, but one specialization in particular – pediatric ICU (PICU) nursing – comes with a unique set of challenges. On the flipside, however, it's hard to find a more rewarding career. Pediatric ICU nurses are often the saving grace in the midst of a family health crisis, helping young patients and their loved ones through physically and emotionally difficult times. With the right expertise and a caring nature to go along with it, PICU nurses can really impact a child's hospital experience, and help aid in his or her recovery.

CERTIFICATIONS: BLS & PALS
(REQUIREMENTS MAY VARY BASED ON FACILITY PREFERENCE)
FEATURES: Works with pediatric patients; high acuity; critical patients; vents and cardiac monitoring
NURSE-TO-PATIENT RATIO: 1:1–2
Subdivisions: None
FLOATING: Not unless specified, not typically for PICU

EXAMPLES OF PATIENTS CARED FOR:

- Respiratory Failure
- Flail Chest
- RDS
- Chest Tube
- Nasal CPAP
- Pulmonary Edema
- Pulmonary Emboli
- GI Bleed
- Sepsis
- GI/Renal Disorders
- Cardiovascular Disease/Disorder
- Neuro/Spine Injury
- CNS Infections
- Post-Abdominal Surgery

Questions to ask an PICU RN: What is the survival rate of ECMO? Do you have experience in acute care floating to NICU? Do you have experience working in acute care setting children's hospital? How much experience do you hold with ECMO?

CARDIAC CATHETERIZATION LAB UNIT: A Cardiac Cath Lab Nurse works with patients who have catheters inserted into the heart for cardiac conditions or defects. The cardiac catheterization lab is an examination area of the hospital that specializes in procedures that allow doctors to visualize specific aspects of the heart. Cardiac catheterizations can be used strictly for diagnostic reasons or for invasive procedures that do not require operating rooms.

CERTIFICATIONS: BLS & ACLS
(REQUIREMENTS MAY VARY BASED ON FACILITY PREFERENCE)
FEATURES: Monitor and circulate cardiac procedures; may also scrub and assist physician with procedure
NURSE-TO-PATIENT RATIO: 1:1
Subdivisions: EP, IR
FLOATING: None

EXAMPLES OF PATIENTS CARED FOR:

- Catheterization
- Angioplasties
- Implant Cardiac Defibrillators
- Pressure Studies
- Insert, Remove, or Replace Pacemaker
- AV Node Ablation
- Rotablation

Questions to ask a Cath Lab RN: What is the difference between Cath lab and EP lab? Are you awake during an EP study? How much experience do you have with IR or EP?

Healthcare Non-Specialty Nursing Areas:

MEDICAL SURGICAL UNIT: In general, M/S nurses provide care and treatment to ill, injured, and recovering adults. The medical-surgical nurse must be able to assess patient condition, administer medications, change dressings, monitor vital signs, keep records, and provide patients with support and education. As a med-surg nurse, you have the opportunity to work in various healthcare settings – hospitals, clinics, nursing homes, and surgical centers – and to treat patients with a wide variety of needs, illnesses, and injuries. In a clinic, nurses often conduct routine physical exams, which allow for a relationship to form between the practitioner and patient. In a hospital, nurses work collaboratively with other healthcare professionals to treat patients with complex diagnoses that often require technology-driven total care. The diverse opportunities available to med-surg nurses have contributed to this field's high desirability and expansive growth. As the largest nursing specialty, Med-Surg nurses now compose one-sixth of all practicing nurses.

CERTIFICATIONS: BLS
(REQUIREMENTS MAY VARY BASED ON FACILITY PREFERENCE)
FEATURES: Various range of patients
NURSE-TO-PATIENT RATIO: 1:5-8
Subdivisions: None
FLOATING: Possibly to Telemetry unit

EXAMPLES OF PATIENTS CARED FOR:

- Post-Surgical
- Diabetics
- Bariatric Surgery

- Ortho
- Detox
- Psych
- Cancer
- Asthma
- Emphysema
- Heart Disease

Questions to ask a Medical Surgical RN: Have you floated to Telemetry unit? Can you read strips & EKG's? Do you have experience changing central line dressing?

TELEMETRY UNIT: Telemetry nursing is a specialization within nursing. These nurses use high-tech equipment to measure life signs, dispense medication, and communicate with patients. Most work in hospitals or similar clinical settings with acute disorders such as heart failure, diabetes, or neurological problems. Telemetry nursing is a specialization within nursing. These nurses use high-tech equipment to measure life signs, dispense medication, and communicate with patients. Most work in hospitals or similar clinical settings with acute disorders such as heart failure, diabetes, or neurological problems.

CERTIFICATIONS: BLS & ACLS
(REQUIREMENTS MAY VARY BASED ON FACILITY PREFERENCE)
FEATURES: Cardiac rhythm monitoring; titrate drips; monitor for cardiopulmonary and respiratory emergencies.
NURSE-TO-PATIENT RATIO: 1:4-5
Subdivisions: PCU, Stepdown, IMCU
FLOATING: Possibly to Medical-Surgical unit

EXAMPLES OF PATIENTS CARED FOR:

- Post-Surgical
- Heart Attack
- CHF
- GI Bleeds
- Renal Failure
- COPD
- Chest Pain
- Diabetics
- Advanced Cancer
- Irregular Heart Rhythm
- Post CABG

Questions to ask a Telemetry RN: Have you floated to Med-Surg or other units? Can you read strips & EKG's? Do you have experience changing central line dressing? How much experience with titrate, drip and cardiac do you have?

PEDIATRICS UNIT: Nurses who specialize in pediatrics devote their knowledge and skills to caring for children from infancy through the late teen years and their families. ... Like other nurses, pediatric nurses can perform physical examinations, measure vital statistics, take blood and urine samples and order diagnostic tests. Nurses who specialize in pediatrics devote their knowledge and skills to caring for children from infancy through the late teen years and their families. These specialized nurses usually complete advanced training in pediatrics and collaborate closely with physicians and other health care providers who share their dedication to children's health.

CERTIFICATIONS: BLS & PALS
(REQUIREMENTS MAY VARY BASED ON FACILITY PREFERENCE)
FEATURES: Similar to Med Surg EXCEPT cares only for pediatric patients; care for a broad array of illnesses/disorders.
NURSE-TO-PATIENT RATIO: 1:3-5
Subdivisions: None
FLOATING: None

EXAMPLES OF PATIENTS CARED FOR:

- Post-Surgical
- Diabetics
- Ortho
- Cancer
- Transplant
- Pneumonia
- Asthma
- Respiratory Disorders

Questions to ask a Peds RN: Do you have any experience in any other units other than Peds?

BEHAVIORAL HEALTH UNIT: Psychiatric mental health registered nurses work with individuals, families, groups, and communities, assessing their mental health needs. The PMH nurse develops a nursing diagnosis and plan of care, implements the nursing process, and evaluates it for effectiveness. Psychiatric Mental Health Advanced Practice Registered Nurses (PMH-APRNs) offer primary care services to the psychiatric-mental health population. PMH-APRNs assess, diagnose, and treat individuals and families with psychiatric disorders or the potential for such disorders using their full scope of therapeutic skills, including the prescription of medication and administration of psychotherapy. PMH-APRNs often own private practices and corporations as well as consult with groups, communities, legislators, and corporations.

CERTIFICATIONS: BLS
(REQUIREMENTS MAY VARY BASED ON FACILITY PREFERENCE)
FEATURES: Patients with mental illness
NURSE-TO-PATIENT RATIO: 1:6-12
Subdivisions: Geriatrics, Adult, Adolescent (Peds)
FLOATING: None

EXAMPLES OF PATIENTS CARED FOR:

- Adolescent
- Adult
- Alcohol/Substance Dependency
- Alzheimer's/Dementia
- Outpatient
- Long-Term
- Suicidal
- Mood Disorders

Questions to ask a Psych RN: Do you have Medical-Surgical or Geriatric experience? Do you work with Peds or Adults? Or both?

ONCOLOGY UNIT: Oncology nurses care for people of all ages who are diagnosed with cancer. Oncology is a challenging field in which nurses support patients, families, and caregivers through the stress of diagnosis and treatment, and the anxiety of many uncertainties brought on by the disease, including facing mortality. Oncology nurses care for people of all ages who are diagnosed with cancer. Oncology is a challenging field in which nurses support patients, families, and caregivers through the stress of diagnosis and treatment, and the anxiety of many uncertainties brought on by the disease, including facing mortality.

CERTIFICATIONS: BLS & OCN
(REQUIREMENTS MAY VARY BASED ON FACILITY PREFERENCE)
FEATURES: Administer and manage chemotherapy; monitor physical conditions; prescribe medication
NURSE-TO-PATIENT RATIO: 1:1–4
Subdivisions: None
FLOATING: None

EXAMPLES OF PATIENTS CARED FOR:

- Pediatric Cancer
- Adult Cancer
- Post-Surgical
- BMT

Questions to ask an Oncology RN: Are you Chemo certified holding OCN certification? Do you have experience floating to Med-Surg? Do you with both adult and peds oncology patients?

Healthcare Certifications: Coast 2 Coast Mentoring LLC.

Healthcare Certifications:

Nursing credentials and certifications are the various credentials and certifications that a person must have to practice nursing legally. In the United States and Canada, many nurses who choose a specialty become certified in that area, signifying that they possess expert knowledge. There are over 200 nursing specialties and subspecialties. Studies from the Institute of Medicine have demonstrated that specialty-certified nurses have higher rates of patient satisfaction, as well as lower rates of work-related errors in patient care. Credentials and certifications focus on keeping healthcare professionals current with common healthcare procedures and varying every one to two years on being renewed. Most common certifications are:

- BLS—Basic Life Support
- ACLS—Advanced Cardiac Life Support
- TNCC—Trauma Nursing Core Course
- PALS—Pediatric Advanced Life Support
- ENPC—Emergency Nursing Pediatric Course
- NRP—Neonatal Resuscitation Program
- NALS—Neonatal Advanced Life Support
- PEARS—Pediatric Emergency Assessment, Recognition, and Stabilization
- AWHONN—Association of Women's Health, Obstetric Neonatal Nurses [AWHONN offers two types of certifications: Advanced Fetal Heart and Intermediate Fetal Heart]
- STABLE—Sugar, Temperature, Airway, Blood Pressure, Lab

Work, Emotional Support (assessment and care modules for critically ill and premature infants)

- **ONC/ONS—Oncology Nursing Association**
- **NIHSS—National Institute of Healthy Stroke Scale**
- **CST—Certified Surgical Technologist**
- **PICC Line—Peripherally Inserted Central Catheter**

It is important to review any and all information in regard to specific state requirements for credentials and licensure. You can search any state online followed by "board of nursing," and you will be directed to that state's formal application process. Inaccurate or incomplete information on the application, Answering "yes" to any of the personal data or background questions, A broken seal on documents from your state of verification or Transcripts, Smudges on the fingerprint cards. Lastly delayed verification of education or license are "ALL" factors that may postpone credentials or licensure.

*** Most healthcare agencies reimburse for certifications, verify if your company does. ***

Healthcare State Licensure Info: Coast 2 Coast Mentoring LLC.

Healthcare State License Information & Details:

A license is a state's grant of legal authority to practice a profession within a designated scope of practice. ... Under a licensure system, states define by statute the tasks and function or scope of practice of a profession and provide that these tasks may be legally performed only by those who are licensed. All RN's must be licensed. Some hospitals are willing to wait for a nurse to acquire licensure depending on how great the need may be and how long it may take. Some states are considered "Walk-Thru" states, meaning you can take all required documents to the board of nursing, and they will provide you a license usually that day.

*** <u>Does your company or agency offer license reimbursement?</u> ***

<u>Healthcare Enhanced Nurse Licensure Compact (eNLC):</u>
The enhanced NLC, or eNLC, which is an updated version of the current Nurse Licensure Compact, allows for registered nurses (RNs) and licensed practical/vocational nurses (LPN/VNs) to have one multistate license, with the ability to practice in both their home state and other eNLC states. Travel nurses often work across state lines, and the Nurse Licensure Compact (NLC), coordinated by the National Council of State Boards of Nursing (NCSBN), makes the process substantially easier to work travel assignments in member states. This is an excellent list of the states in the original NLC, but a new version of the compact, which has been ratified by NCSBN in 2015, has now been enacted. The revised compact, called the enhanced Nurse Licensure Compact (eNLC), went into effect on July 20, 2017, when North Carolina became the 26th state to sign its provisions into law. Even as more states agree to the new provisions and join the eNLC, representatives from the original states who make up the Interstate Commission will oversee the compact's implementation in the coming months. The commission members set Friday, January 19, 2018, as the official implementation date for the enhanced NLC. If you have any questions about the enhanced NLC, compact nursing licenses, or how to get your nursing license in a non-compact state, contact the recruiters and licensing experts with our partner travel nursing agencies. The eNLC adopted 11 uniform licensure requirements

(ULRs) in order for an applicant to obtain a multistate license. One of those requirements is submission to federal and state fingerprint-based criminal background checks (CBCs). More information can be found at www.ncsbn.org. In order for states to become part of this new eNLC program, state legislature has to meet and vote on it. If approved, it then must pass the state senate and finance committee and must then be signed by the state governor.

*** Which states are part of the enhanced NLC?

Here is the current list of states that have enacted the enhanced Nurse Licensure Compact:

- Alabama
- Arizona
- Arkansas
- Colorado
- Delaware
- Florida
- Georgia
- Idaho
- Iowa
- Kansas
- Kentucky (joining in July 2019)
- Louisiana (joining in July 2019)
- Maine
- Maryland
- Mississippi
- Missouri

- Montana
- Nebraska
- New Hampshire
- New Mexico
- North Carolina
- North Dakota
- Oklahoma
- South Carolina
- South Dakota
- Tennessee
- Texas
- Utah
- Virginia
- West Virginia
- Wisconsin
- Wyoming

*** What is the Enhanced Nurse Licensure Compact?

Allowing nurses to have mobility across state borders, the enhanced NLC increases access to care while maintaining public protection. The enhanced NLC, or eNLC, which is an updated version of the current Nurse Licensure Compact, allows for registered nurses (RNs) and licensed practical/vocational nurses (LPN/VNs) to have one multistate license, with the ability to practice in both their home state and other eNLC states. All states, including those participating in the existing NLC, must introduce legislation in the coming years to enter into the eNLC. Patient safety concerns have led to the addition of new features in the provisions of the legislation of the enhanced NLC. Licensing standards are aligned in enhanced NLC states so all applicants for a multistate nursing license are required to meet the same standards, which include a federal and state criminal background check that will be conducted for all applicants applying for multistate licensure.

Healthcare Key Components to Apply for Licensure:

Licensure is the process by which boards of nursing grant permission to an individual to engage in nursing practice after determining that the applicant has attained the competency necessary to perform a unique scope of practice. Licensure is necessary when the regulated activities are complex and require specialized knowledge and skill and independent decision making. The licensure process determines if the applicant has the necessary skills to safely perform a specified scope of practice by predetermining the criteria needed and evaluating licensure applicants to determine if they meet the criteria. It vital if necessary, to provide assistance in the process to relieve stress which will gain rapport. Assist by following these guidelines:

- Complete the application for endorsement. Found on the state's board of nursing website, make sure to follow and complete every detailed instruction.
- Purchase the state license fee and temporary licensure to begin work while waiting for permanent license in mail.
- Go to www.NURSYS.com and follow NURSYS verification. Nursys.com provides online verification for endorsement to a nurse requesting to practice in another state and anyone who wants to verify a nurse license. Primary source equivalent: The Nursys licensure and disciplinary database is the repository of the data provided directly from state boards of nursing. Note not all states participate. Complete the steps under the "NURSYS Nurse License Verification for Endorsement" page,

which cost thirty dollars. It releases the license information for the state you have selected to another.

- Secure verification from original state of licensure if state is not listed on NURSYS. The form of verification is attached with the application. RN will need to fill-in their portion in full details and send remaining documents to the original licensing state's board of nursing.
- Acquire verification of transcripts from school. RN need to call the staff office at the school and request those transcripts. School staff should provide you with an application or form to complete. Either mail or fax in.
- Execute a background check with no actions or hit against license.
- Fingerprints may be conducted and completed through Livescan in the state RN is applying. The plus to Livescan are results is relayed quicker, often within three days. If not, you will need to obtain a blue federal fingerprint card with ink fingerprints completed at any local police department. Also, some states have particular fingerprinting cards so check with each state to verify.

Healthcare State RN License Information Compact States:
Nursing License Compact States

*Indicates awaiting implementation

1. **Alabama – 3 days to 1 week/temp – 1-2 weeks/perm**
2. **Arizona – "Walk Thru" – 2 weeks by mail or 48 hours walk thru/temp – 1-2 months/perm**
3. **Arkansas – 2-4 weeks/temp – 1 month/perm**

4. Colorado – 4-5 weeks/temp – 6 weeks/perm
5. Delaware – 2-6 weeks/temp – 2-6 weeks/perm
6. Florida – 3-4 weeks/temp – 4-6 weeks/perm
7. Georgia – no temp – 2-4 weeks/perm
8. Idaho – 2 weeks/temp – 2 months/perm
9. Indiana* – 2 weeks/temp – 4-6 weeks/perm
10. Iowa – no temp – 15 days/perm
11. Kansas – 7-10 days/temp – 1 month/perm
12. Kentucky – 2-4 weeks/temp – 2-4 weeks/perm
13. Louisiana – 2-3 weeks/temp – 4-6 weeks/perm
14. Maine – 7-14 days/temp – 2-3 months/perm
15. Maryland – 2-3 weeks/temp – 4 weeks/perm
16. Mississippi – no temp – 7-10 days/perm
17. Missouri – 2-3 weeks/temp – 2-3 weeks/perm
18. Montana – no temp – 30 days/perm
19. Nebraska – no temp – 2-4 weeks/perm
20. New Hampshire – 4 weeks/temp – 4 weeks/perm
21. New Jersey* – 2-3 weeks/temp – 6-8 weeks/perm
22. New Mexico – no temp – 2-3 weeks/perm
23. North Carolina – 1-2 weeks/temp – 4-6 weeks/perm
24. North Dakota – 3-4 days/temp – 3-4 days/perm
25. Oklahoma – 2 weeks/temp – 2 weeks/perm
26. South Carolina – 1-2 days/temp – 14 days/perm
27. South Dakota – 2-3 days/temp – 4-6 weeks/perm
28. Tennessee – no temp – 6 weeks/perm
29. Texas – 2-3 weeks/temp – 2-3 weeks/perm
30. Utah – no temp – 7-21 days/perm
31. Virginia – 30-day Auth to practice letter/temp – 4-6 weeks/perm
32. West Virginia – 3-5 days/temp – 7-10 days/perm

33. Wisconsin – 2 weeks/temp – 2-3 weeks/perm
34. Wyoming – 3-5 days/temp – 90 days/perm

Healthcare State RN License Information:
Healthcare Non-Compact States:

1. Alaska – 10 days to 1 week/temp – 10 days/perm
2. California – no temp – 8-12 weeks/perm
3. Connecticut – 10-15 days to 1 week/temp – 3-4 months/perm
4. D.C. – 1-2 days/temp – 1-2 months/perm
5. Hawaii – same day/temp – 2-3 weeks/perm
6. Illinois – 4 weeks/temp – 4-6 weeks/perm
7. Massachusetts – no temp – 4-6 weeks/perm
8. Michigan – no temp – 2-3 months/perm
9. Minnesota – 5 days /temp – 5 days/perm
10. Nevada – 1-2 weeks/temp – 2-4 months/perm
11. Ohio – 1-2 weeks/temp – 2-3 weeks/perm
12. Oregon – no temp – 4-6 weeks/perm
13. Pennsylvania – 12-14 days/temp – 12-14 days/perm
14. Vermont – no temp – 3-5 days/perm
15. Washington – 2-3 weeks/temp – 8 weeks/perm
16. Rhode Island no temp – 8 weeks/perm
17. New York no temp – 3-6 weeks/perm

Healthcare Non-Specialty Nursing Units:

LTC/LTAC (Long-Term Care/Long-Term Acute Care): Long-term care nurses care for patients who have an illness or condition that requires care for an extended period of time. Often working with the elderly or patients with disability, long-term care nurses work in nursing homes, long-term care facilities and rehabilitation centers. A long-term acute care facility is a specialty-care hospital designed for patients with serious medical problems that require intense, special treatment for an extended period of time—usually 20 to 30 days.

Hospice: A hospice nurse is a specialist in the nursing field who is trained to work closely with terminally ill patients. While nurses who work in hospice settings are licensed as a registered nurse, they play a special role as a case manager and advocate for patients who are nearing the end of their life and their families.

Dialysis: Dialysis nurses are part of a larger specialty known as nephrology nursing, and they have an in-depth knowledge of kidney disease. They support, medicate, and monitor patients throughout dialysis as well as educate them on kidney disease and the lifestyle choices that help them to manage their disease

Rehabilitation: The rehabilitation nurse is a nurse who specializes in helping people with disabilities and chronic illness attain optimal function, health, and adapt to an altered lifestyle. Rehabilitation nurses assist patients in their move toward independence by setting realistic goals and treatment plans.

LPN (Licensed Practical Nurse): The role of an LPN will vary depending on where you work, and your state might even put regulations on the types of duties you're allowed to perform. That said, a licensed practical nurse job description frequently includes: Maintaining patient records Measuring vital signs Administering and monitoring medication Assisting doctors and nurses with tests and procedures Helping patients eat, dress, and bathe Updating doctors and nurses on patient status LPNs working in the maternity ward of a hospital have additional duties that include feeding infants and coaching women through childbirth.

CNA (Certified Nursing Assistant): Certified Nursing Assistants (CNAs) assists patients with various activities in hospitals, nursing homes, and other medical facilities. They are responsible for activities such as bathing, dressing, and checking vital signs. Certified Nursing Assistants (CNAs) assists patients with various activities in hospitals, nursing homes, and other medical facilities. They are responsible for activities such as bathing, dressing, and checking vital signs. They also administer medications, reposition patients who are bedridden, and collect information about treatment plans.

HH (Home Health): Home Care Nurses provide care to patients in their homes under the guidance of a physician. They perform regular visits where they monitor the patient's condition, assess their wounds, and change dressings as required. Home Care Nurses also write reports and communicate with the doctor after each visit.

Healthcare Allied Health Units:

Radiology: A Radiology Technician works with a Radiologist to diagnose and treat patients using diagnostic imaging examinations like X-rays, CT scans, and MRI scans. The Radiology Technician will prepare patients and equipment for radiology procedures, perform the tests, and maintain the equipment

- **X-ray**: Nonvisible X-rays create an image of internal structures and organs.
- **CT (Computed Tomography):** An advanced X-ray exam that takes digital images of the body. Using very high speed computers, CT scans create a 360-degree image like an X-ray. It produces many images of the body as if sliced like a loaf of bread.
- **MRI (Magnetic Resonance Imaging):** MRIs depict bone as well as soft tissue in the body. An MRI, with such high resolution, can give physicians images that can help visualize cartilage, tendon pathology, nerves, and other soft tissue structures in the body.
- **Mammo (Mammography):** A mammogram is a type of X-ray equipment used specifically to take images of women's breasts and locate tumors
- **Ultrasound:** Ultrasounds use very high frequency sound waves to produce images. Often associated with pregnancy, ultrasounds are now often used to find soft tissue abnormalities around joints, tendons, and muscles.
- **Echo (Echocardiogram):** An Echo is an ultrasound specific to the heart. It is used to look at the heart's structure and check how well the heart is working.

PT/PTA (Physical Therapist/Physical Therapy Assistant): Physical therapists help people with physical injuries or illnesses of to regain range of movement and control their pain. ... They help determine the root causes of the trauma, counsel patients, and work with them to create a plan for rehabilitation. Under the direction and supervision of physical therapists, physical therapist assistants treat patients through exercise, massage, gait and balance training, and other therapeutic interventions. They record patients' progress and report the results of each treatment to the physical therapist.

OT (Occupational Therapist): Occupational therapists treat disabled, ill or injured patients with special equipment and the therapeutic use of daily activities. They help patients improve, regain and develop the skills needed for day to day life and work. They may provide long-term patient care and acute patient care.

RT (Respiratory Therapist): Respiratory therapists typically do the following: Interview and examine patients with breathing or cardiopulmonary disorders. Consult with physicians to develop patient treatment plans. Perform diagnostic tests, such as measuring lung capacity.

MT/MLT (Medical Technologist/Medical Laboratory Technician): Medical technologists conduct laboratory tests, procedures, experiments, and analyses to provide data for diagnosis, treatment, and prevention of disease. They analyze bodily fluids like blood, urine, and spinal fluid, to determine the presence of normal and abnormal components. Medical lab technicians prepare samples for analysis, use equipment to locate microorganisms, monitor tests and procedures, analyze the chemical content of fluids, match blood for transfusions, and test for drug levels in the blood.

Radiation Therapist/Dosimetrist: Radiation therapists operate machines, such as linear accelerators, to deliver concentrated radiation therapy to the region of a patient's tumor. Radiation treatment can shrink or remove cancers and tumors. Radiation therapists are part of the oncology teams that treat patients with cancer. Dosimetrists are health professionals in charge of planning radiation treatment for oncology patients. In collaboration with other members of the oncology team, they also oversee treatment implementation while providing support with radiation equipment.

Phlebotomist: Phlebotomists are professionals who specialize drawing blood from patients. Their responsibilities include interviewing and preparing the patient for the blood draw. Phlebotomists then label the blood sample and take it to the laboratory for testing.

CHAPTER 3

Healthcare Hospital Introduction – Coast 2 Coast Mentoring LLC.

Categories of Hospitals:

Critical Access Hospital: Critical Access Hospital is a designation given to eligible rural hospitals by the Centers for Medicare and Medicaid Services (CMS). The CAH designation is designed to reduce the financial vulnerability of rural hospitals and improve access to healthcare by keeping essential services in rural communities. These hospitals are typically small with beds counts never exceeding twenty-five. 24/7 Emergency Room acute care is required. Floating to multiple units is usually required.

General or Community Hospital: Community hospitals provide an embedded, relational model of care within which the functional, social, interpersonal and psychological aspects of patient experience are all integral. There are, however, considerable variations in support both across and within communities and over time. Community Hospitals are small local hospitals that provide a range of services to their local community. These can include community beds, maternity, clinics, minor injuries units, X ray departments and much more. ... Community hospitals vary considerably, as they have adapted to the needs of their local populations. These hospitals are not part of a large teaching facility, healthcare systems or chain of independent hospitals. Bed counts vary from 25 to 350 beds.

Teaching/Academic Hospital: A teaching hospital, or academic medical center, is a hospital that partners with medical and nursing schools, education programs and research centers to improve health care through learning and research. Academic medical centers and teaching hospitals fulfill critical social missions, including educating and training future medical professionals; conducting state-of-the-art research; caring for the poor and uninsured; and optimizing services to provide highly specialized clinical care to the most severely ill and injured patients. Many advances and develop new technology with revolutionary research that improves illnesses and quality of life. Bed counts often exceed 500 beds.

Magnet Awarded Hospitals: The designation of "Magnet Hospital" is awarded by the American Nurses Credentialing Center (ANCC). This coveted honor helps hospitals attract patients, nurses, and other medical staff. Before achieving Magnet status, a hospital must demonstrate excellence in nursing and patient care as well as innovation in professional nursing practice. Out of the top 20 hospitals on the Best Hospitals Honor Roll 2017–2018, 17 are Magnet hospitals. There are currently 461 Magnet hospitals in the United States, and only 8.28 percent of all U.S. hospitals have Magnet status. The Magnet Model To achieve Magnet status, hospitals must demonstrate a high standard of excellence in five areas: Transformational leadership: Supporting and advocating for patients and staff and having strong nursing leaders at every level. Structural empowerment: Recognizing the contributions of nursing staff, committing to professional development, and decentralizing decision-making. Exemplary professional practice: Showing competence and accountability in professional procedures, systems, and practices. Systemically measuring care and outcomes is also essential. New knowledge, innovations, and improvements: Requiring research and evidence-based practice to be incorporated into operational and clinical processes. Encouraging innovation throughout the organization is important as well. Empirical outcomes: Emphasizing community, patient, workforce, and organizational outcomes. Hospitals need a combination of time and resources to receive Magnet status. Achieving this status takes an average of 4.25 years and costs approximately $2.1 million. However, Magnet hospitals gain an average of $1,229,770 to $1,263,926 in increased revenue per year and can recoup their investment within two years of being accredited. In 1983, the American Academy of Nursing (AAN) Task Force on Nursing Practice in Hospitals conducted a study to identify attributes of organizations that recruit and retain qualified nursing staff. In 1990, the AAN approved the Magnet Hospital Recognition Program for Excellence in Nursing Services, using the 1983 study as a framework. In 1994, the University of Washington Medical Center in Seattle was named the first ANCC Magnet-designated organization. The goal of Magnet status is to identify and systematize nursing excellence, as excellence in nursing can lead to better patient outcomes. Magnet hospitals tend to have a low patient-to-nurse ratio, lower mortality rates for surgical patients, lower hospital-associated infection rates, and a shorter average length of stay for stroke patients. Patients being cared for in Magnet hospitals have a 21 percent lower likelihood of receiving a hospital-acquired pressure ulcer and an 8.6 percent lower mortality rate after a postoperative complication. They also have a 5 percent lower probability of falling while in the hospital's care. Magnet status is associated with a variety of benefits. It advances nursing standards, cultivates a collaborative culture, improves the hospital's reputation and financial outlook, leads to the recruitment and retention of highly qualified healthcare professionals, and increases the standard of patient care, safety and satisfaction.

Healthcare Assets and Links:

American Hospital Directory (www.ahd.com). Site frequently used by agency staff to gather information about a hospital, including size, address, phone number, trauma designation, and teaching status.

American Trauma Society (amtrauma.org). Site used to locate trauma-designated facilities throughout the United States.

Healthcare Fundamental Hospital Vocabulary:

Staffing

- *Centralized staffing:* One department is responsible for staffing all units, including call-in staff, call-off staff, and float staff.
- *Decentralized staffing:* Charge RNs, managers determine the level of staffing needed before and during the shift.

Unit design

- *Centralized:* The nursing station is centrally located and serves as a hub within the unit.

- Decentralized: Nursing stations are often located directly outside patient rooms. Serve to decrease walking distances and improve patient visibility.

Types of staffing models incorporated by hospitals

- *Budget based:* This looks at the number of nursing hours per patient day. It looks at the average number of patients per twenty-four-hour period on a unit and determines how many nurses they will need to accommodate. It does not make considerations for influx of patients or times of low census.
- *Nurse-patient ratio:* This is based on how many patients a single nurse can care for on a given unit. While most hospitals adhere to a national average for nurse-to-patient ratios, hospitals that use this staffing model do not always account for changes in patient acuity levels and the extra time a nurse may need to spend with patients.
- *Patient acuity:* This model is based on how complex the care is for a patient. It determines the time that goes into caring for patients based on their health conditions and assigns staffing accordingly.

Healthcare Grading of Nursing Team Structure:

Chief Nursing Officer (CNO): The Chief Nursing Officer is a wearer of many hats who works with other healthcare leaders to establish policies that benefit nursing staff and improve clinical care. A CNO will likely be involved in advising senior management on best nursing practices, creating retention programs, establishing compensation wages, managing nursing budgets, planning new patient services, conducting performance assessments, and representing nurses at board meetings. Chief Nursing Officers often spearhead personnel management, which means implementing the recruitment, hiring, and retention processes. CNOs manage the staff working in multiple nursing departments in their health system, but still must report to the facility's Chief Executive Officer.

House Supervisor: A nurse supervisor is responsible for managing staff, overseeing patient care and ensuring adherence to established policies and procedures. She is charged with assigning staff and monitoring their activities, and with helping to recruit and train new personnel. The nurse supervisor also acts as an interface between her staff, their patients, and the patients' families, as well as between her staff and the hospital's physicians. Administrative duties are another sizable part of her responsibilities. Chief Nursing Office is their superior.

Director of Nursing: Directors of nursing are nurse administrators who work at hospitals, nursing homes and other healthcare facilities. Their duties might include supervising the nursing staff and overseeing patient care as well as administrative functions such as record keeping and budgeting. At minimum, they need a diploma, associate's or bachelor's degree in nursing, along with a current state nursing license. Many employers want directors of nursing with master's degrees in nursing or healthcare administration.

Nurse Manager/Supervisor: Nursing supervisor jobs focus on achieving critical clinical healthcare goals, with an emphasis on improving patient care delivery, quality, and outcomes. Essential responsibilities in a typical nursing supervisor job description include managing nursing staff and establishing policies and procedures for effective patient care. Nursing supervisor jobs also involve directly interacting with patients and their families in clinical settings. Like their nursing staff, nursing supervisors are dedicated advocates for patients. Often working alongside staff nurses in treating patients, nursing supervisors are keenly aware of patient concerns. When nurses are unable to share patient observations with physicians, nursing supervisors represent nursing staff and report their findings. They are the Lead nurse in unit specialty.

Charge Nurse: Charge nurses are responsible for overseeing a specific department within a healthcare facility for their assigned shift. Individuals in this role perform such duties as delegating nursing assignments, preparing schedules, overseeing admissions and discharges, and monitoring and ordering medicines and supplies. In addition to these managerial tasks, charge nurses also may carry a patient load depending on where they work and their shift.

Staff Nurse: A staff nurse is supposed to manage patient care and subsequent recovery. Staff nurses work on helping individuals who have undergone injuries, from illnesses to accidents. Staff nurses are on most occasions the first healthcare professionals that one is likely to encounter when a visit to a hospital or any other healthcare facility becomes a necessity. Before a doctor or a nurse practitioner arrive, staff nurses usually assess a patient's condition while taking vital reports so that the doctor can assess the patient more thoroughly. Under the orders of the doctor, a staff nurse will administer medications and injections in addition to helping doctors in the process of diagnostic testing. Staff nurses are a part of aftercare as well, whether that means educating the patients about what to do after leaving the hospital or preparing patients for discharge. Staff nurses coordinate and provide patient care alongside doctors and nurse practitioners; they are also essential to providing patients and family members with information and providing emotional support and advice.

Healthcare Hierarchy of Nursing Team Pyramid:

1. **Chief Nursing Officer (CNO)**
2. **House Supervisor**
3. **Director of Nursing Services**
4. **Nurse Manager**
5. **Charge Nurse**
6. **Staff Nurse**

Healthcare Electronic Medical Records (EMR) Charting Systems:

A digital version of the traditional paper-charting medical record for an individual patient is known Electronic Medical Records (EMR). EMR is a healthcare vocabulary term used to describe the software exercised by hospital.

Most common EMR systems used by hospitals and healthcare systems across the nation:

- **EPIC**
- **Cerner**
- **MediTech**
- **Soarian**
- **McKesson**
- **Sunrise**

- **Allscripts**
- **eCinicalWorks**

It's vital to understand how much experience healthcare candidates have with each EMR system, whether or not healthcare candidate has experience. Note some hospital and healthcare systems have EMR systems molded exclusively to that client. Make sure to tell possible candidates, that's it is best to be orientated to that charting system when available especially if candidate has no experience. You never want to put your candidates in a position to lose. Give them the best chance possible being your money rides on it.

Healthcare Hospital RN Testing Requirements:

When it comes to hospital RN testing's each hospital or hospitals systems are different. Clients may request certain testing prior to start of assignment. Familiarize yourself with each hospital RN testing's, therefore you able to prep your candidates and set each other for success. What's best for the candidate, is always best for you as well. You are a team. Examples of testing that could be required by hospitals are:

Online Nurse Competency Testing: Nursing competency includes core abilities that are required for fulfilling one's role as a nurse. Therefore, it is important to clearly define nursing competency to establish a foundation for nursing education curriculum. However, while the concepts surrounding nursing competency are important for improving nursing quality, they are still not yet completely developed. Thus, challenges remain in establishing definitions and structures for nursing competency, competency levels necessary for nursing professionals, training methods and so on. In the present study, we reviewed the research on definitions and attributes of nursing competency in Japan as well as competency structure, its elements and evaluation. Furthermore, we investigated training methods to teach nursing competency. That being said, online nurse competency testing is utilized by staffing agencies and healthcare systems across the country. Some of the benefits using online nurse competency testing are reduction of cancelation or terminations, reduced orientation and a greater quality healthcare candidate.

Performance Based Development System or PBDS: It's an exam hospital use to conduct on property. Your candidate contract rides on passing exam, or the contract will be ended immediately. The Performance-Based Development System (PBDS) evaluates a nurse's ability to think critically in various clinical situations. More and more of our clients are using the PBDS Test as a way to evaluate clinician competency and to standardize their orientation process. PBDS is comprised of multiple videos healthcare candidates must watch. Once the video has been reviewed, healthcare candidate must recall the steps to grasp the patient-care situation displayed on video. Candidate must be detailed, list step by step in exact order. Attention to detail is extremely important. Agencies should provide candidate with prep material in order to pass exam.

Healthcare Hospital Traveler Orientation:
Orientation for nurses in hospitals can vary from facility to facility and even unit to unit. The best you can do is to ready any required documents, complete your paperwork and/or modules in advance, arrive early, and be prepared to soak up as much information as you can. There is no typical travel nurse orientation. In order to assist your healthcare candidates best, know particulars of each hospitals orientation process

to provide service to your candidates most wouldn't. This will create a solid working foundation between you and healthcare candidate, as well as build rapport. Each Hospital orientation schedules are not the same, but these general parts provide the structure for a successful orientation.

- **Human Resources:** Candidate typically meets first with HR team at hospital upon arrival to assignment. HR Team will have candidate complete new-hire forms with consist of employee hospital handbook, privacy policies, HIPPA documentation along with a few others.
- **EMR Training:** Candidate will meet with instructors to gain experience in order to learn the EMR system used by healthcare facility. EMR training lasts around one to two days.
- **Hospital Orientation:** An engaging hospital orientation programs sets the scene for new nurse hires to thrive in the workplace. They combined and streamlined nursing orientation programs at three hospitals to make them standardized, consistent, and uniform. During orientation the candidate will go over hospital policies and procedures involving patient care, patient safety, privacy and emergency situations such as earthquakes, fire and natural disasters.
- **Unit Introduction:** Specialty areas will require additional training. The focus of the unit orientation is unit-specific competencies and to provide the nurse with patient care opportunities that enable them to demonstrate competence. Candidate needs to learn the layout of the unit and get familiar with locating supplies needed to provide the best patient care possible. Candidate needs to understand what is expected of the unit with respect to admissions and discharges, patient coding,

medication waste discharge, ordering of medications, visitation hours, policies and procedures are a few examples. An experienced staff healthcare worker will follow you during the initial unit orientation, so you may ask questions and learn a greater understanding of the unit. Keep an open line of communication with your candidate throughout this process to make sure they everything they need. Support is crucial. This will reduce the possibility of candidates being fired or quitting. It important to ensure as best as possible, candidate has a positive experience.

Communications with Healthcare Hospitals:

A healthcare account manager works as a liaison between a client and a medical hospital or organization. The duties of someone in this sales position are to complete sales of products or services and undertake contract negotiations when needed. How the account manager communicates with a client facility may be impacted by the contractual relationship between the agency and facility. These differences exist depending on the relationship an agency has established with hospital.

– **Direct Contracts:** Direct arrangements with providers are implemented to lower overall costs by improving pricing transparency and eliminating "middle-men" entities, which in today's environment can be significant barriers for better managing healthcare. Advantages of direct contracts offer contact with the decision-makers with each unit eliminating the run-around frustrations. Direct contracts allow more flexibility in negotiating hospital bill rates, eliminates vendor fees, and speedy onboarding process.

- **Vendor Management System (VMS):** Vendor management is the process that empowers an organization to take appropriate measures for controlling cost, reducing potential risks related to vendors, ensuring excellent service deliverability and deriving value from vendors in the long run. So, that's where the vendor management system or VMS comes in place. A Vendor Management System (VMS) is an internet-based software application that enables a business to procure and manage temporary and permanent staff as well as contract and contingent staff. The Vendor Management System usually includes: Staff ordering processes or job requisition. Automated billing. When direct contract is not acquired a hospital and agency could enter an agreement through Vendor management system (VMS) FieldGlass, Shiftwise, Medefis, AYA Connect, Vizient, WAND, Focusone Solutions are a few Vendor Management Systems. Vendor Management Systems are supposed to be vendor neutral. The purpose is supposed to eliminate perks obtained by some agencies to ensure the most qualified candidates are reviewed no matter what agency they are representing. Communication with hospital staff through VMS is often frustrating and difficult. It's important for account managers to establish trust and reliability with hospitals contracted though VMS to increase the chances of your candidates receiving offers.

- **Managed Service Provider (MSP):** A managed services provider (MSP) is most often information technology (IT) services provider that manages and assumes responsibility for providing a defined set of services to its clients either proactively or as the MSP (not the client) determines that services are needed. Managed Service Provider is not vendor neutral. A Managed

Service Provider provides rights to a specific agency or group of agencies and offers competitive advantage to the agency in exchange for management of all staffing needs. Eliminating the need for facilities to manage billing for multiple agencies and removing the need to communicate with multiple account managers for the great number of agencies they contracted with. Agencies may have MSP accounts themselves or may be sub-vendors. Communication can be extremely advantageous for the agency that possesses the MSP but offers the complete opposite to sub-vendors and/or noncontracted agencies wishing to pursue a contractual relationship with the client facility.

– **Healthcare Hospital Organizations:** Each state has a hospital association representative. Hospitals have the right to become a member or not. Hospital associations usually assign a representative in charge of keeping the line of communication open with agency vendors to fill staffing needs. There is some negotiation with rate structures due to a lawsuit filed in past, but rates are mostly fixed once they are secured in. Disadvantages to The Hospital Association Agreement are untimely or limited communication, decreased control of the sales process and lower rates to name a few examples. Large number of contracts as well as fixed pricing to ensure no under cutting are examples of advantages of The Hospital Association Agreement.

CHAPTER 4

Healthcare Recruiting Business: Coast 2 Coast Mentoring LLC.

Healthcare Recruiting Business

When it comes to producing or creating production is very important to learn how your company obtains leads to produce business. You need learn how your company generates leads? How does your agency distribute those leads? Some leads are stronger than others. It's important to determine which ones are better and why? You need to know how your hospitals and MSP/VMS systems are managed by account managers. Investigate what Customer Relationship Management (CRM) software your company uses. Customer relationship management (CRM) is a technology for managing all your company's relationships and interactions with customers and potential customers. The goal is simple: Improve business relationships. A CRM system helps companies stay connected to customers, streamline processes, and improve profitability. Verify if your company's CRM have the following functions and learn to utilize.

- Importing New Leads
- Setting Follow-Ups
- Social Media Settings
- Rate Calculator
- Submission Tracking
- Profile Functions
- Running Queries
- Seizing Notes
- Best Time to Contact
- Emailing or Texting from the CRM
- Job Entry/ Search Functions
- Onboarding and Documentation Process
- Call Guidelines
- Performance Tracking and Key Performance Indicators

CHAPTER 5

Generating Voice Messages: Coast 2 Coast Mentoring LLC.

Generating Voice Messages:

80 percent of unknown calls go directly to voicemail. It's crucial to leave a lasting impression to create a response. We will discuss a plan of action on how to leave effective voice messages. Leaving optimal voice messages will separate you from other recruiters. Choose your words wisely. Depicting on your words used can distinguish between a voice mail being returned or not. Over 70 percent of voice mails returned are based on tone. Make sure to be energetic, confident and speak clearly. It's vital to make sure you're not speaking too quickly or slowly. Speak at an even pace. Keep your tone neutral and smooth. Be in a comfortable state. Regulate your voice to project positive vibes. When your confident, you speak in a natural tone. If you are uncomfortable, your pitch is higher. Great recruiters are confident and comfortable when leaving voicemails. Make sure to keep your voice messages within 30 seconds. Keep them short, sweet and to the point. Make sure to address the purpose of your call most importantly.

Advice for Recruiters Leaving Voice Message:

Set yourself apart from your competition. Keep in mind candidates are being bombarded daily with calls from other recruiters. Some agencies have notes in the system on candidates. Use those notes to your advantage. For instance, "Hi Candidates Name! Hope you're having a blessed day; I noticed your looking for Labor and Delivery in compact states for night shift. A job just became available molding your requirements and reach out and see if you still interested. If so please contact me as soon as possible so I may provide the full details, answer any questions you may have. If you deem at that point the job is feasible please email resume, unit certifications and two references. Once received, unit skills checklist will be assigned. Once completed let's get you submitted and seal an offer." Make sure to sound positive and upbeat.

Another method that is effective is to lead with enticing question. This question should be direct to the candidate to initiate a response. Great example would be, "Hi Candidate Name, have you struggled to find work in rural locations as PEDS RN? A lot of candidates were experiencing the same frustrations, until they received my services. When free please contact or email me to discuss solutions on how my service could cater and mold your needs. I will follow up shortly to see when is best to talk being jobs fill fast. Take the time to create and perfect your voicemail and email blasts.

CHAPTER 6

Healthcare Sales Overview: Coast 2 Coast Mentoring LLC.

Healthcare Sales Cycle Overview:

Five basic steps are included in the healthcare industries sales cycle. Each step must be methodically performed as it builds into the following. Recruiters must qualify candidates to verify and ensure the best candidates are being sent to hospitals. Account managers must certify the hospitals to make certain the candidate has a successful assignment. Members of your team need to work cohesively to ensure successful job matching between hospitals and candidates. Establishing clear agendas for both the candidate and hospital make closing deals easier and provides a better customer experience for everyone.

In the next chapters it will detail on each of the five steps in the healthcare industries sales cycle. The execution of each step can be molded and adjusted to fit your style or preference. Never comprise the integrity of each step. They provide key details for developing rapport to successful offers. The process of the five steps are listed below in order.

1. Qualifying Candidate
2. Creating Value
3. Pay Packages and Job Order Matching
4. Negotiating and Closing to Seal Deals
5. Onboarding and Experience

CHAPTER 7

Qualifying your Healthcare Travelers: Coast 2 Coast Mentoring LLC.

Qualifying your Healthcare Candidates

Screening Potential Candidates:

Finding qualified candidates molding the hospitals requirements is extremely important. Candidates have vital jobs to occupy. It's your responsibility to ensure the best possible patient care is being provided to your hospitals. People lives are at stake and that is not to be taken lightly.

Asking lots of detailed questions is how to qualify potential candidates. Make sure your questions require candidate to provide details and stray from "yes" or "no" responses.

Examples:

- – What are your travel requirements and expectations?
- – How many years do you have work in an acute care hospital setting?

- What unit specialties do you have experience with?
- What units have you floated to and have experience in?
- What is your shift preference?
- What traits are you looking for in a company and recruiter?
- How did you learn of company?
- What made you interested in traveling?
- What trauma level or levels do you have experience in?
- Where are you licensed in?
- What active certifications do you hold?
- What patio ratios do you feel comfortable working with?
- What bed size counts are you used to?
- When are you looking for work currently or upcoming and do you need to give notice?
- What locations are you looking to explore?
- When you travel, who do you travel with?
- What are you looking to take home weekly?
- What benefits are you possibly interested in?
- What other agencies do you work with?
- What is the way to contact and communicate with you?
- Are there any questions or concerns you would like me to address?
- Have you travel before? If so, what are your thoughts? What are the pros and cons?

Red Flags and the Importance of Qualifying:

Once the candidate and hospital have signed contract confirmations the onboarding/compliance process takes place. The candidate at this time gets fully credentialed. Medical records must be up to date and on hand, employment verifications have been processed, background and drug screens have been cleared and any other documents required have been met by agency or hospital.

The process of qualifying candidates can cost lots of money for the agency and hospital. It's the agencies obligation to the hospital or hospitals you are representing to provide the most suitable candidate on the market. As a recruiter, you're their lifeline and it's important to advocate for your nurses. Beware of red flags early in the recruitment cycle. A red flag in the healthcare industry is a warning sign that's your candidate is possibly not qualified for the position. Acknowledging and removing red flags can be hard and time consuming.

When offers are retracted it is typically traced back to a red flag warning in the qualifying process that was overlooked or disregarded. Asking specific questions of candidates will help discover and pint out those red flags. It's your job to conduct a detailed research to verify if the candidate is the best possible fit. You're not going to close every offer. Trust your instincts.

Healthcare Red Flags Potentials:

- Gaps in employment
- Hits on License
- Hits on background
- Prescription Medications
- Trouble retrieving references
- If they have to get approval from a spouse
- Job Hopping
- Poor Communication
- Not sending documents in a timely manner
- Not answering or returning phone calls

- If they are aggressive to start asap. Question why?
- Issues with previous agency or recruiter

Healthcare Common Objections:

Displayed are several examples of objections most commonly used and how-to rebuttal them. You want to ask two to three questions for every candidate statement.

I've heard from other travelers that I can make more money
Rebuttals:

Be careful and do research to verify that the rate posted is accurate and correct. Some agencies use bait tactics in order to get candidates in database. Also, some agencies don't distinguish unit specialties or correct shifts. Whether they offer travel reimbursement, 401k, insurance and other benefits as well as make sure if they are included in a blended rate or not.

Understood, what agency are they with? You want to make sure your comparing a feature by feature comparison. Having knowledge of your competition is huge and will separate you from the rest of recruiters.

Are you willing to work an extra shift or do a 48-hour guaranteed contract?
Are they quoting weekly or hourly?
What's taxable versus tax free?

My other agency pays more
Rebuttals:

We can negotiate pay within feasible measures. What is the other agency offering? May you send me a copy of package so I may compare.

Does the agency have a direct contract? Your agency might pay a little more but that doesn't mean they will seal an offer for you. Our account managers have a great rapport with this hospital and will make sure your profile is reviewed and get you an interview. It's up to you at that point to seal the offer.

Looking to stay close to home and need to be in a specific location for my upcoming assignment
Rebuttals:

What is your travel radius you allotting me to work with to determine what opportunities mold your requirements?

I possibly have a hospital in area but have heard terrible reviews on the travel groups. Which is more vital job security or location?

If I could offer you money at another hospital would you consider? Is money a determining factor in your decision making?

How long are you willing to hold out until a position opens up molding your requests?

If you were able to schedule block shifts and were able to travel home when needed, would you consider a contract outside your preferred radius?

I'm satisfied with my current agency and recruiter
Rebuttals:

Understood, but it's always great to have other options being I might have a job and location where you desire, and your current agency doesn't.

How long have you been with them? What are some do you like and dislike about your current agency?

When I have Crisis or Elevated pay rates would you like me to reach out? If your recruiter or agency ever disappoints or doesn't meet your standards, please do not hesitate to contact me.

Healthcare Recruiting Call Sheet:

Name: _____

Cell #: _____

Email: _____

Permanent Home Address: _____

Preferred Method of Contact? _____

Current Specialty: _____ Years of Experience: _____

Secondary Specialty: _____ Years of Experience: _____

Total Years of Experience: _____

Date Available: _____

Shift Preference: _____

Hospital/Unit Bed Size/Patient Ratios: _____

Priorities for Traveling:_____

Compact License: _____

Active State License: _____

Inactive State License: _____

Original State of License: _____

Certifications:

__ ACLS __ AWHONN

__ BCLS __ STABLE

__ CCRN __ Fetal Heart

__ TNCC __ PICC Line

__ ENPC __ NIHSS

__ NRP __ NALS

__ PALS __ PEARS

Specialty

ER:

Trauma levels worked?

Peds exp?

Average bed size?

ICU:

Willing to float?

Average bed size?

Subset experience? MICU, SICU, CVICU

ART lines?

Balloon pumps?

Sheath removal?

CVP?

CRRT?

Adult ECMO?

LVAD?

OR:

Scrub?

Circulate?

Specialized areas?

First assist?

Call?

Average cases per day?

PACU:

Pre-/Post-op?

ICU post-op?

Chest tubes?

Extubating/re-Intubating?

Types of surgeries?

Peds?

LDRP:

High risk?

Postpartum?

Antepartum?

Nursery?

OB?

Mother/Baby?

Circulate c-sections?

Cath Lab:

IR experience?

EP experience?

NICU:

Level?

Oscillators?

ECMO?

Non-Specialty

Med Surg:

Float?

Read strips?

Post-op patients?

Central line changes?

Accessing ports?

Wound vacs?

Telemetry/PCU/Stepdown:

Float?

Titrate drips?

Cardiac exp?

Pull sheaths?

Post cath patients?

Use a FemoStop?

1-day CABG patients?

Pulled pacer wires?

PICU/Peds:

Children's hospital?

Patient population?

Psych:

Peds?

Geriatric?

Long-term floor?

Short-term floor?

Oncology:

Hospital experience?

Cancer center exp?

Chemo cert?

Peds?

OR Tech:

Certified?

Unit size exp?

Specialized areas?

Call?

Cases per day?

CHAPTER 8

Qualifying Your Hospital: Coast 2 Coast Mentoring LLC.

Qualifying Your Hospital:

Healthcare Screening Questions:

To learn more about your hospital and ways to increase the value you could provide. Do not hesitate to ask questions immediately being it will only benefit. The more details you know about the hospital will help solve problems and earn a spot-on preferred list of agencies. Not to mention it will prep you to match the most qualified candidates for your hospital open job orders. Examples are of screening questions are provided below.

- – **Which agencies do you typically use?**
- – **What makes that agency a great fit to work with?**
- – **What are weaknesses you see in agencies you work with?**
- – **What do your expectations in agencies when entering a new partnership?**

- What EMR charting system does your hospital use?
- What are the details of your orientation process?
- What unit specialties are hardest for your hospital to fill? Are you able to provide an increase bill rate? Any room for flexibility on those hard to fill positions?
- Do you extend your travelers? Find out why? Or why not?
- How long have your used healthcare travelers?
- What unit departments use travelers the most? Are they usually for night shift or does it vary? Is floating required and if so for what unit specialties?
- Who decides on offers?
- When it comes to phone, text or email what do you prefer?

Healthcare Hospital Red Flags:

Screen your hospitals as you would with potential candidates. Your agency's creditability is just as vital as the reputation with hospitals. Stay alert for these few things.

- Billing Issues
- Invoicing Issues
- Large turnaround of travelers
- The client becomes desperate and overlooking require-ments, therefore lowering the quality of the traveler
- Failure to communicate
- The job requisition has been open for a long period of time
- Testing being administered with a large failure rate

When revealing red flags with hospital make sure to clear any con-cerns in a polite manner. Whatever you do just ensure you're not being confrontational by any means. You always what to stay on hospital best side. You want to be able to get help to iron out those concerns. If you are having an issue with communication, supply the hospital with solutions that are useful and ensure them that you are there to cater their needs. Ask to text directly if you have urgent issues that need immediate answers.

Healthcare Common Objections:

Its tough breaking through to hospitals. Objections are guaranteed when trying to open new business especially when first introducing yourself and agency. You have to realize they are busy and get bombarded with calls constantly. Below are a few objections that are most common that you will probably hear and what questions to respond with.

Your agency rates are too high!

Questions to ask back to hospital decision maker:
At your current bill rate are you filling job orders?
Are you getting qualified candidates at that rate?
What about experimenting with a higher bill rate temporarily to see if position fills quick?
Would you consider guarantying 48-hour guaranteed contract with the reduce rate?

We are part of an MSP/VMS System

Questions to ask back to hospital decision maker:
How has the partnership of VMS/MSP system working? What are pro's and con's?

Who is the VMS/MSP that you use?

How much time do you provide VMS/MSP to fill your job orders before you release to agencies?

What are the estimated percentages of you maintain being managed by MSP/VMS?

Is every department contracted through the MSP/VMS?

When does you MSP/VMS contract expire?

Are you considering continuing your MSP/VMS partnership once contract expires?

We already have too many contracts

Questions to ask back to hospital decision maker:

Are your agencies filling job orders to your satisfaction?

If you are unsatisfied with the production of an agency, what requirements would need to be met to form a partnership?

What are the positives with the current agencies you are working with?

Are there any adjustments you would make with current agencies?

We only welcome new business annually or once every couple of years

Questions to ask back to hospital decision maker:

Are you receiving value from your current agencies?

If your agencies that you are currently contracted with can't supply adequate production would you consider adding new agencies to replace those underperforming?

Census is low and we are trying to reduce our travelers

Questions to ask back to hospital decision maker:

What system do you have in place for hiring travelers if a crisis arises?

What is your hospital doing differently than most to prevent employing travelers?

What resources do you have in place if by coincidence you need to hire travelers immediately?

CHAPTER 9

Creating Value for Your Traveler: Coast 2 Coast Mentoring LLC.

Solving Problems and Identifying Opportunities:

As we know wisdom is priceless and knowledge is power. Some unit manager can't comprehend the value of travelers so it's best to educate them if they are willing to lend an ear. Unit managers duty is to help with hospitals bottom line.

Hospital reimbursements are dependent on lower readmissions and quality patient care. Are hospitals missing money opportunities? When a job order is left open on units, how long until they consider utilizing travelers? Around fifty percent of travelers experience high levels of burn out and exhaustion. The cost of hiring travelers versus staff average almost evenly. One in four travelers plan on leaving their jobs in next two years. When it comes to the national average, travelers job dissatisfaction is five times higher. Higher patient mortality rates are due to poor staffing.

You are probably pondering, "How does hiring staff cost equivalent as employing a traveler?" Many sources have noted once the hospital includes fees for health, vision and dental benefits, workers compensation, malpractice and liability insurance, paid vacation and acquired sick pay, matching of 401k, relocation, sign-on bonus, tuition and social security, the hourly funds are within a couple dollars of a traveler bill rate. Employing travelers saves them money overall being they don't have to carry the burden of paying money during times of low census.

Benefits of forming a Partnership:

What are the benefits of partnering up with your agency? The highest value is having you as an account manager! What is the hospital going to receive from your agency that sets you aside from your competitors? You must create value to build rapport in order to be an asset to that hospital. You need to set yourself apart from your competition or there is no reason for your services. Below are examples of methods that will separate you from other recruiters.

- **What's your reputation with your hospitals and what are they stating about your agency?**
- **How strong does quality process?**
- **Does your agency have high retention of travel staff? Stronger job-matching process and quality of profiles is what it means.**
- **Does your agency have and experience recruitment team?**
- **Is your agency simplifying invoice's?**
- **What is your agency's reputation with other hospitals?**

CHAPTER 10

Creating Value for Your Client: Coast 2 Coast Mentoring LLC.

Requirements of Healthcare Hospitals:

The hospital will reach out when job orders develop, so make sure you retrieve full descriptions and details of the assignment and the job order they are looking to fill. These questions below are vital in supplying full details to healthcare candidates, in order to verify if the job order molds their experience. These questions are important to get answered to supply your healthcare candidates adequately.

- What EMR system does hospital utilize?
- What are the shifts details?
- Are Scrubs provided? If not, what color are the hospitals scrubs?
- When is the start date?
- Is shift 8, 10, or 12 hours?
- Is floating required? If so, to what unit or units?
- What is patient ratio to nurse?

- What certifications are required?
- What is the bed & unit sizes of your units?
- Do you have exam requirements?
- Is on-call required? If so, what are the details to on-call?
- Are block shifts available or every other weekend?
- Do you have any scheduling restrictions?
- How long is orientation and what's it composed of?

Matching Healthcare Candidates:

Hospitals rely heavily on agencies during the placement cycle. Make sure your candidate profiles are organized with attention to the details. Sending qualified candidates will earn higher rapport then other agencies, therefore getting you awarded on hospital's preferred list. Well-built profiles are exactly what hospitals look for and will make the overall interview process simple.

At this time in your partnership, you should know precisely what your hospitals are looking for in candidates and submission profiles. It's a must to overview submission profiles at least three times and if able have a peer review as well. You need to ensure there are no mistakes, so your profile is not rejected to be sent back for revision. Your candidate, therefore, would lose that slot in the submission order. Extremely important to verify your candidate is the best possible match and most qualified for the job order. Observe for red flags throughout the recruiting cycle, like RN not having experience recently within that unit specialty you are submitting to, if candidate has worked at small hospitals its probably not best to work at large unit sized hospital off the bat. If candidate is accustomed to low patient ratio counts it would be difficult for that nurse to complete a job order to a job that has seven to one patient ratios. If you have any questions discuss with your team to determine whether the candidate is truly qualified and in the best interests of your hospital and traveler. Reputation is huge in the healthcare industry and word of mouth spreads fast.

It's your duty to assist hospitals in filling job orders and "NOT" your responsibility to make decisions on behalf of the hospital. If you ever receive candidate submission profiles that mold what the hospitals are looking for, yet not available until a certain date or possibly a different shift, send the submission profile anyways. Always let the hospital decide being it never hurts. Agencies have received many offers through this recruiting tactic.

Never say you are coming to overdeliver. Would be a costly mistake that can be avoided, plain and simple. Under promise is the best strategy. Set a fair standard, then exceed and crush it. With healthcare hospitals personally take the time to review all submission profiles before sending, by displaying your strongest candidates ahead of weaker. Offer to set-up phone interviews as well as prescreens to verify they are the best possible match before sending to hospital.

Healthcare Candidate Profile Review:

As discussed, it is vital to produce strong candidates molding your hospitals requirements. How do you know if your candidate molds the requirements of your hospital? You want to have this checklist below perfected to ensure your profile is complete with attention to the details. This gives you that separating toll versus others.

- Analyze resume, skills checklist, certifications and references for any errors or red flags
- Verify that requested time off has been included if candidate has requested
- Do they have all the required certifications and RN state license required by hospital?
- Have they worked in similar unit size and bed size hospitals?
- Verify the candidate is 200% ready to accept an offer before submitting
- Ensure pay packages were discussed
- Ensure candidate is fully aware of start date and is 100% able to start at that date
- Verify if candidate needs insurance
- Makes sure the candidate meets skills set requirements listed by hospital
- Determine if candidate will work on-call
- Clarify the shift and hours per shift to ensure no hiccups
- Make sure RN license is current
- Make sure no hits or action against background
- Disclose hits against a nurse license to hospital if you discover any. Will be rapport and trust.

What Healthcare Hospital Expect from Agencies:

Out the gate you what to establish what separates you from others to hospitals. Why can hospitals rely on versus others?

This is your time to showcase your traits. If you are energetic, loving, punctual, hard worker, organized, loyal or other qualities, make sure to display those traits in every call to separate yourself apart from your competitors. Know your hospitals requirements and plant those in your pitch when calling candidates. Express how your benefits and strengths will impact them in a positive way. Instead of stating, I pay attention to the details, "use, "Hospitals who partner with me have a trouble-free time with compliance and onboarding process which leads to candidates staring assignments on time."

Hospitals aren't directly work with your agency, they are interacting with you, so sell yourself versus agency. You are the person holding their hand throughout the process and their advocate. Make sure to know what differentiates you from others. Be an original, not a photocopy.

CHAPTER 11

Steps to Packaging Together Healthcare Profiles: Coast 2 Coast Mentoring LLC.

Putting Healthcare Submission Profile Together:

What is a Submission Profile?

A healthcare submission profile is a combined packet of candidate information your agency sends to hospitals when a traveler is interested in a job order. The information composed in a submission packet is the healthcare industry standard and is required by all hospitals. Profiles consist of the following:

- Profile or cover letter
- Resume – Must be update and any employment gaps over thirty days need to be explained
- License Verification
- Unit Certifications – Depending on unit certain certifications are required to work in that specialty

- – Two references (recent within one year) – must be Charge, Manager, Supervisor or Director
- – Unit Skills Checklist

How to create a Lasting Profile/Cover Letter:

Early in the training manual refer to the types of nurses and mold key phrases alongside unit skills checklist. Take key words from the job order and utilize them. For example, if a hospital requests an ER nurse with pediatric experience, make sure to point out those strengths in the skill set section of the profile cover letter. A few examples below.

"Noah Is a strong ER RN with eight years acute care pediatric emergency room hospital setting experience. Three of those years have been recent travel experience within a children's level one trauma hospital. Candidate is fully credential which would make compliance smooth, quick and stress-free. Candidate is actively licensed in your state with no hits or action against license and ready to orientate as soon as possible if granted an offer. This candidate molds every listed requirement and has vast experience. Candidate has heard great reviews about your hospital and is excited for the opportunity to possibly join you team."

"Lisa is a seasoned Progressive Care & Telemetry RN who has no issues floating to multiple units vast experience with several EMR systems including EPIC, Cerner, McKesson & MediTech. She is a critical thinker able to adapt at a moment notice. Her supervisors rave about her skills sets within unit. Lisa loves working in fast pace environments, always willing to help co-workers without being asked. Lisa is excited to possibly join your hospital. She is available to interview and start today.

Make sure to perfect your cover letter being that is the first document that is seen. Investigate the cover letter to ensure no errors or inaccurate information, being this simple error could result in your candidate being rejected. Always review for red flags and accuracy before sending to hospital.

Displayed below is a sample of a how a polished submission profile looks.

Date _____ 06/17/2020

CANDIDATE INFORMATION
Candidate: Michelle Kimberly Neal
Candidate phone: (345)123-4567
Available to Start: ASAP
Specialty: L&D

Candidate email: michelle@gmail.com
Time off Request: None

EXPERIENCE
Years Experience - Total: 25+
Certifications: *BLS/ACLS/NRP*
Computerized Charting Experience: Yes
Has Candidate every worked for client in the past (Y/N)? Yes

Years Experience in Specialty: 25+
Lic. State/Number/Expiration: CA/951356789 Exp. 1-31-23

APPLICATION QUESTIONS
Eligible to Work in US (Y/N)?
Has license every been revoked (Y/N)?
Convicted of a Felony/Misdemeanor (Y/N)?
Defendant in a Liability Action (Y/N)?
Currently employed with Lead (Y/N)?
Recruiter confirmed candidate is OK to float (Y/N)?
Recruiter confirmed candidate can start their own IV's (Y/N)?

SUMMARY OF PROFILE
Resume with sufficient experience in specialty
Checklist
References
Proof of active & valid license

BOARD OF REGISTERED NURSING - BRN
LICENSING DETAILS FOR: 416877

NAME: NEAL, MICHELLE KIMBERLY
LICENSE TYPE: REGISTERED NURSE
PRIMARY STATUS: CURRENT
ADDRESS NOT DISCLOSED

ISSUANCE DATE
JANUARY 1, 1987

EXPIRATION DATE
JANUARY 31, 2021

CURRENT DATE / TIME
MARCH 29, 2020
4:23:26 PM

DISCIPLINARY ACTIONS

THERE ARE NO DISCIPLINARY ACTIONS AGAINST THE LICENSE.

PUBLIC RECORD ACTIONS

ADMINISTRATIVE DISCIPLINARY ACTIONS (NO RECORDS)

COURT ORDER (NO RECORDS)

LICENSE ISSUED WITH PUBLIC LETTER OF REPRIMAND (NO RECORDS)

AUTO DISCLOSURE (NO RECORDS)

PUBLIC DOCUMENTS (NO RECORDS)

101

Michelle Kimberly Neal
L&D RN - 25+ Years of experience in High-Risk L&D
(C) (345) 123-4567
Michelle@gmail.com

WORK HISTORY

Riverside Community Hospital – Riverside, CA   11/2019 – Present
Travel RN – L&D
      Facility Bed Size : 350
      Unit Bed Size: 14 - 300 deliveries a month
      Patient Ratio: 2:1
      Patient Population:
      EMR: Cerner

Bakersfield Memorial Hospital – Bakersfield, CA   09/2019 – 11/2019
Travel RN – L&D
      Facility Bed Size : 400
      Unit Bed Size: 14 - 300 deliveries a month
      Patient Ratio: 2:1
      Patient Population:
      EMR: Cerner

Rancho Springs Medical Center – Murrieta, CA   06/2019 – 09/2019
Travel RN – L&D
      Facility Bed Size : 120
      Unit Bed Size: 12 - 250 deliveries a month
      Patient Ratio: 2:1
      Patient Population:
      EMR: Cerner

San Antonio Regional Hospital – Upland, CA   03/2018 – 06/2019
Travel RN – L&D
      Facility Bed Size : 363
      Unit Bed Size: 10 - 250 deliveries a month
      Patient Ratio: 2:1
      Patient Population:
      EMR: Cerner

Loma Linda University Hospital – Murrietta, CA   01/2018 – 03/2018
Staff RN – L&D
      Facility Bed Size: 110

    Unit Bed Size: 8 - 80 deliveries a month
    Patient Ratio: 2:1
    Patient Population:
    EMR: Cerner

Rancho Springs Medical Center – Murrieta, CA   01/2017 – 01/2018
Travel RN – L&D
    Facility Bed Size: 120
    Unit Bed Size: 12 - 250 deliveries a month
    Patient Ratio: 2:1
    Patient Population: Pre-Labor, Intra-Labor, Post-Labor, Newborn Infant, High-Risk
    EMR: Cerner

Garden Grove Hospital – Garden Grove, CA   08/2016 – 01/2017
Travel RN – L&D
    Facility Bed Size: 175
    Unit Bed Size: 12 - 80 deliveries a month
    Patient Ratio: 2:1
    Patient Population: Pre-Labor, Intra-Labor, Post-Labor, Newborn Infant, High-Risk
    EMR: EPIC

Huntington Memorial Hospital – Pasadena, CA   04/2014 – 07/2016
Travel RN – L&D
    Facility Bed Size: 619
    Unit Bed Size: 12 - 230 deliveries a month
    Patient Ratio: 2:1
    Patient Population: Pre-Labor, Intra-Labor, Post-Labor, Newborn Infant, High-Risk
    EMR: Cerner

St. Bernardine Medical Center – San Bernardio, CA   01/2013 – 03/2014
Travel RN – L&D
    Unit Bed Size: 14 - 300 deliveries a month
    Patient Ratio: 2:1
    Patient Population: Pre-Labor, Intra-Labor, Post-Labor, Newborn Infant, High-Risk
    EMR: Centricity

01/2012 - 01/2013 - Took off a year to go on vaction and take care of househouse

Kaiser Permanente Medical Center – Anaheim, CA   12/1993 – 12/2011
Travel RN – L&D
    Facility Bed Size : 262
    Unit Bed Size: 18 - 400 deliveries a month

Patient Ratio: 2:1
Patient Population: Pre-Labor, Intra-Labor, Post-Labor, Newborn Infant, High-Risk
EMR: EPIC

St. Mary's Medical Center – Long Beach, CA   01/1990 – 12/1993
Staff RN – L&D

South Coast Medical Center – Laguna Beach, CA   01/1988 – 12/1989
Staff RN – L&D

South Coast Medical Center – Garden Grove, CA   01/1987 – 01/1988
Staff RN – L&D

EDUCATION

Rancho Santiago College – Orange, CA
A.D.N. 05/1987

LICENSURE AND CERTIFICATIONS
Licensed RN California #472257   Exp. 07/2020
ACLS   Exp. 04/2021
BLS   Exp. 11/2020
NRP   Exp. 09/2020
AWHONN   Exp. 03/2021
Fire-Safety Card   Exp. 01/2021

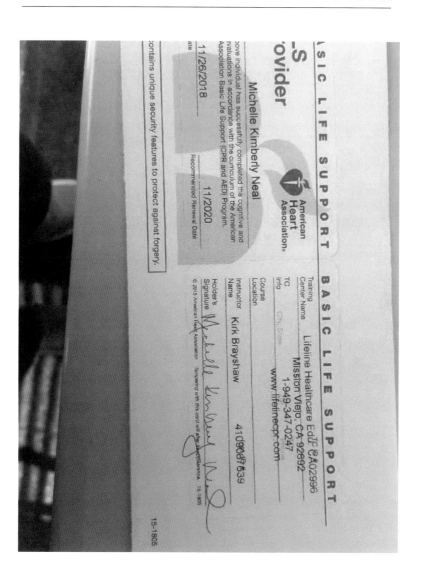

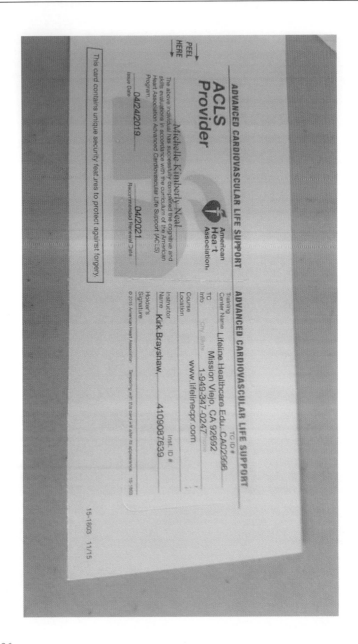

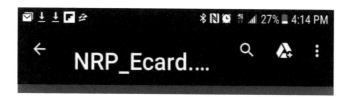

Neonatal Resuscitation Program (NRP)
PROVIDER

The individual named below has successfully completed the national cognitive and skills evaluations in accordance with the NRP curriculum of the American Academy of Pediatrics and American Heart Association

Michelle Kimberly Neal
Provider Name and Credentials

3/27/2019	3/31/2021
Course Completion Date	Recommended Renewal Date

If you have any question regarding the NRP, please contact the American Academy of Pediatrics life support staff at 800/433-9016, option 4, by e-mail at lifesupport@aap.org or online at www.aap.org/nrp.

This NRP e-card can be sent to any third party by e-mail. The cardholder must return to his or her online NRP account to designate the recipient's address.

This card signifies completion of the following lessons:

Lesson 1: Foundations of Neonatal Resuscitation
Lesson 2: Preparing for Resuscitation
Lesson 3: Initial Steps of Newborn Care
Lesson 4: Positive-Pressure Ventilation
Lesson 5: Alternative Airways: Endotracheal Tubes and Laryngeal Masks

Lesson 6: Chest Compressions
Lesson 7: Medications
Lesson 8: Post-resuscitation Care
Lesson 9: Resuscitation of Babies Born Preterm
Lesson 10: Special Considerations
Lesson 11: Ethics and Care at the End of Life

American Academy of Pediatrics

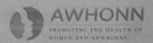

Michelle Kimberly Neal
9376 Cerra Vista St.
Apple Valley, CA 92308

CONTINUING NURSING EDUCATION CERTIFICATE

Michelle Kimberly Neal

has completed the activity titled

Advanced Fetal Monitoring Course

on January 6, 2019

ACCREDITATION STATEMENT(S)

AWHONN is accredited as a provider of continuing nursing education (CNE) by the American Nurses Credentialing Center's Commission on Accreditation.

AWHONN also holds a California provider number: CEP580.

This program has been granted 8.00 contact hours.

Donna Ruth, MSN, RN

Donna Ruth, MSN, RN
Director, Educational Services
AWHONN
1800 M Street NW, Suite 740 South
Washington, DC 20036

Verify at: info.awhonn.bespce.com/vf.php?x=8UMOrcuAPORImy

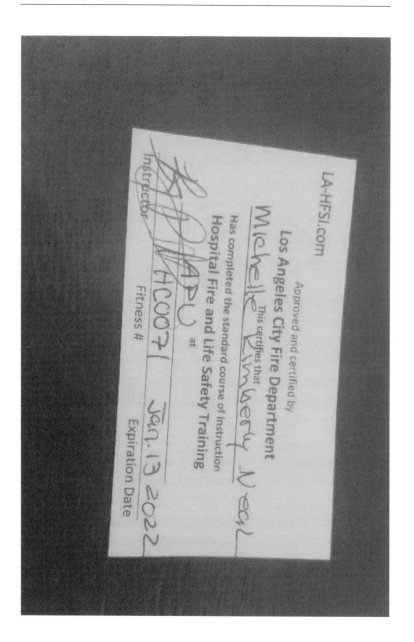

LA-HFSI.com

Approved and certified by

Los Angeles City Fire Department

This certifies that

Michelle Kimberly Neal

Has completed the standard course of instruction

Hospital Fire and Life Safety Training

at

Instructor

HC0071   Jan. 13 2022

Fitness #   Expiration Date

Name of Applicant	Michelle Kimberly Neal			SSN Last 4 digits	
Name of Employer	Riverside Community Hospital		City, State	Riverside, CA	
Job Title / Position	Travel RN	Worked charge?	☐ Yes ☑No		
Unit / Dept	Labor and Delivery	Dates employed	11/2019	To	Present
Name & Title of person providing reference	Emily Procko - Charge RN			Avg hrs/wk	36
Reference Phone	(951) 788-3000	Reference e-mail or fax			

Please rate the candidate using a 5 point scale where 5 equals Superior Performance, 3 equals Meets Expectations and 1 equals Performance Well Below Expectations. I'll ask for your rating in 14 categories.

Performance Ratings > Performance Measures V	NK NA	Superior Performance 5	Exceeds Expectations 4	Meets Expectations 3	Below Expectations 2	Well Below Expectations 1
1 Clinical Knowledge		x				
2 Clinical Judgment		x				
3 Respect & Compassion		x				
4 Teamwork & Cooperation		x				
5 Communication Skills			x			
6 Quality of Work & Documentation		x				
7 Use of Time & Resources		x				
8 Initiative / Motivation			x			
9 Emergency Management		x				
10 Response to Direction & Feedback			x			
11 Policy & Procedure Compliance		x				
12 Punctuality & Dependability		x				
13 Professional Appearance		x				
14 Professional Behavior		x				

NK = Not Known   NA = Not Applicable

Is the position title listed correctly? ☑ Yes ☐ No   Are the dates of employment correct? ☑ Yes ☐ No

Was this a travel or agency assignment? ☑ Yes ☐ No   Would you consider this person for rehire? ☑ Yes ☐ No

Jobsite description: (Patient types, average census, facility # of beds, common diagnoses/procedures)

Applicants strengths-weakness-comments:

Reason for leaving this position:

Do you authorize release of this reference information to the Applicant? ☑ Yes ☐ No

Recruiter/staff who obtained reference	Noah Neumiller	Date Obtained	03/29/20
Date of applicant authorization	03/29/20	Authorization Method	☑ Phone ☐ Fax ☐ Email

Name of Applicant	Michelle Kimberly Neal			SSN Last 4 digits		
Name of Employer	Bakersfield Memorial Hospital		City, State	Bakersfield, CA		
Job Title / Position	Travel RN		Worked charge?	☐ Yes ☑No		
Unit / Dept	Labor and Delivery		Dates employed	09/2019	To	11/2019
Name & Title of person providing reference	Jennifer Anderson - Charge RN			Avg hrs/wk	36	
Reference Phone	(661) 327-4647	Reference e-mail or fax				

Please rate the candidate using a 5 point scale where 5 equals Superior Performance, 3 equals Meets Expectations and 1 equals Performance Well Below Expectations. I'll ask for your rating in 14 categories.

Performance Ratings > Performance Measures V	NK NA	Superior Performance 5	Exceeds Expectations 4	Meets Expectations 3	Below Expectations 2	Well Below Expectations 1
1 Clinical Knowledge		x				
2 Clinical Judgment		x				
3 Respect & Compassion		x				
4 Teamwork & Cooperation		x				
5 Communication Skills			x			
6 Quality of Work & Documentation		x				
7 Use of Time & Resources		x				
8 Initiative / Motivation			x			
9 Emergency Management		x				
10 Response to Direction & Feedback			x			
11 Policy & Procedure Compliance		x				
12 Punctuality & Dependability		x				
13 Professional Appearance		x				
14 Professional Behavior		x				

NK = Not Known   NA = Not Applicable

Is the position title listed correctly? ☑ Yes ☐ No   Are the dates of employment correct? ☑ Yes ☐ No
Was this a travel or agency assignment? ☑ Yes ☐ No   Would you consider this person for rehire? ☑ Yes ☐ No

Jobsite description: (Patient types, average census, facility # of beds, common diagnoses/procedures)

Applicants strengths-weakness-comments:

Reason for leaving this position:

Do you authorize release of this reference information to the Applicant? ☑ Yes ☐ No

Recruiter/staff who obtained reference	Noah Neumiller	Date Obtained	03/29/20
Date of applicant authorization	03/29/20	Authorization Method	☐ Phone ☐ Fax ☐ Email

Name of Applicant	Michelle Kimberly Neal		SSN Last 4 digits	
Name of Employer	Rancho Springs Medical Center	City, State	Murrieta, CA	
Job Title / Position	Travel RN	Worked charge?	☐ Yes ☑ No	
Unit / Dept	Labor and Delivery	Dates employed	06/2019 To 09/2019	
Name & Title of person providing reference	Kristina Killingsworth - Charge RN		Avg hrs/wk	36
Reference Phone	(951) 696-6000	Reference e-mail or fax		

Please rate the candidate using a 5 point scale where 5 equals Superior Performance, 3 equals Meets Expectations and 1 equals Performance Well Below Expectations. I'll ask for your rating in 14 categories.

Performance Ratings > Performance Measures V	NK NA	Superior Performance 5	Exceeds Expectations 4	Meets Expectations 3	Below Expectations 2	Well Below Expectations 1
1 Clinical Knowledge		x				
2 Clinical Judgment		x				
3 Respect & Compassion		x				
4 Teamwork & Cooperation		x				
5 Communication Skills			x			
6 Quality of Work & Documentation		x				
7 Use of Time & Resources		x				
8 Initiative / Motivation			x			
9 Emergency Management		x				
10 Response to Direction & Feedback			x			
11 Policy & Procedure Compliance		x				
12 Punctuality & Dependability		x				
13 Professional Appearance		x				
14 Professional Behavior		x				

NK = Not Known   NA = Not Applicable

Is the position title listed correctly? ☑ Yes ☐ No   Are the dates of employment correct? ☑ Yes ☐ No
Was this a travel or agency assignment? ☑ Yes ☐ No   Would you consider this person for rehire? ☑ Yes ☐ No

Jobsite description: (Patient types, average census, facility # of beds, common diagnoses/procedures)

Applicants strengths-weakness-comments:

Reason for leaving this position:

Do you authorize release of this reference information to the Applicant? ☑ Yes ☐ No

Recruiter/staff who obtained reference	Noah Neumiller	Date Obtained	03/29/20
Date of applicant authorization	03/29/20	Authorization Method	☑ Phone ☐ Fax ☐ Email

Name of Applicant	Michelle Kimberly Neal			SSN Last 4 digits	
Name of Employer	San Antonio Regional Hospital		City, State	Upland, CA	
Job Title / Position	Travel RN		Worked charge?	☐ Yes ☑ No	
Unit / Dept	Labor and Delivery		Dates employed	06/2019 To	09/2019
Name & Title of person providing reference	Venus Phillips - Manager			Avg hrs/wk	36
Reference Phone	(909) 985-2811	Reference e-mail or fax			

Please rate the candidate using a 5 point scale where 5 equals Superior Performance, 3 equals Meets Expectations and 1 equals Performance Well Below Expectations. I'll ask for your rating in 14 categories.

Performance Ratings > Performance Measures V	NK NA	Superior Performance 5	Exceeds Expectations 4	Meets Expectations 3	Below Expectations 2	Well Below Expectations 1
1 Clinical Knowledge		x				
2 Clinical Judgment		x				
3 Respect & Compassion		x				
4 Teamwork & Cooperation		x				
5 Communication Skills			x			
6 Quality of Work & Documentation		x				
7 Use of Time & Resources		x				
8 Initiative / Motivation			x			
9 Emergency Management		x				
10 Response to Direction & Feedback			x			
11 Policy & Procedure Compliance		x				
12 Punctuality & Dependability		x				
13 Professional Appearance		x				
14 Professional Behavior		x				

NK = Not Known   NA = Not Applicable

Is the position title listed correctly? ☑ Yes ☐ No   Are the dates of employment correct? ☑ Yes ☐ No
Was this a travel or agency assignment? ☑ Yes ☐ No   Would you consider this person for rehire? ☑ Yes ☐ No

Jobsite description: (Patient types, average census, facility # of beds, common diagnoses/procedures)

Applicants strengths-weakness-comments:

Reason for leaving this position:

Do you authorize release of this reference information to the Applicant? ☑ Yes ☐ No

Recruiter/staff who obtained reference	Noah Neumiller	Date Obtained	03/29/20
Date of applicant authorization	03/29/20	Authorization Method	☑ Phone ☐ Fax ☐ Email

Candidate: Michelle Kimberly Neal
Discipline: RN - Traveler
Checklist: Labor and Delivery
Date Signed: 02/28/2020

Proficiency		Frequency	
[1] None		[1] Never/Observed Only	
[2] Intermittent		[2] Less than 6 times/year	
[3] Experienced		[3] Twice a Month	
[4] Supervise/Teach		[4] Daily - Weekly	

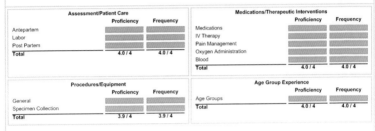

Assessment/Patient Care
	Proficiency	Frequency
Antepartem		
Labor		
Post Partem		
Total	4.0 / 4	4.0 / 4

Medications/Therapeutic Interventions
	Proficiency	Frequency
Medications		
IV Therapy		
Pain Management		
Oxygen Administration		
Blood		
Total	4.0 / 4	4.0 / 4

Procedures/Equipment
	Proficiency	Frequency
General		
Specimen Collection		
Total	3.9 / 4	3.9 / 4

Age Group Experience
	Proficiency	Frequency
Age Groups		
Total	4.0 / 4	4.0 / 4

Electronically Signed by Michelle Kimberly Nea
l ClearSign Technolog on 02/28/20

114

Michelle Kimberly Neal, RN - Traveler   **Labor and Delivery**

Using the scale(s) below, please complete the following skill self assessment based upon your experience within the last 2 years.

Proficiency (1) None (2) Intermittent (3) Experienced (4) Supervise/Teach
Frequency (1) Never/Observed Only (2) Less than 6 times/year (3) Twice a Month (4) Daily - Weekly

Assessment/Patient Care

	Proficiency 1 2 3 4	Frequency 1 2 3 4
Antepartem		
General		
Admission	✔(4)	✔(4)
Amniotic Fluid Index	✔(4)	✔(4)
Assess for Comfort	✔(4)	✔(4)
Breathing/Relaxation Techniques	✔(4)	✔(4)
Coaching	✔(4)	✔(4)
Labor		
General		
Auscultate Fetal Heart Rate (Doppler)	✔(4)	✔(4)
Auscultate Fetal Heart Rate (Fetoscope)	✔(4)	✔(4)
Contraction Characteristics	✔(4)	✔(4)
Deep Tendon Reflexes	✔(4)	✔(4)
Determine Fetal Position	✔(4)	✔(4)
Dilation	✔(4)	✔(4)
Document FHR Patterns	✔(4)	✔(4)
Edema	✔(4)	✔(4)
Effacement	✔(4)	✔(4)
Fetal Presentation/Position	✔(4)	✔(4)
Internal Monitor	✔(4)	✔(4)
Patient Education - Fetal Movement Counts	✔(4)	✔(4)
Perform Admission Risk Assessment	✔(4)	✔(4)
Stages of Labor	✔(4)	✔(4)
Station	✔(4)	✔(4)
Status of Membranes	✔(4)	✔(4)
Toxicology Studies	✔(4)	✔(4)
Uterine Activity	✔(4)	✔(4)
Conditions/Diseases		
Chlamydia	✔(4)	✔(4)
Group B Strep	✔(4)	✔(4)
Herpes	✔(4)	✔(4)
Complications		

Assessment/Patient Care Continued

	Proficiency 1 2 3 4	Frequency 1 2 3 4
Abruptio Placenta	✔(4)	✔(4)
Asthma	✔(4)	✔(4)
Cardiac Disease	✔(4)	✔(4)
Chronic Hypertension	✔(4)	✔(4)
Diabetes	✔(4)	✔(4)
Eclampsia	✔(4)	✔(4)
HBV	✔(4)	✔(4)
Hemolytic Anemias	✔(4)	✔(4)
Hemorrhage	✔(4)	✔(4)
HIV	✔(4)	✔(4)
Hypertension	✔(4)	✔(4)
Malpresentations	✔(4)	✔(4)
Multiple Gestation	✔(4)	✔(4)
Placenta Previa	✔(4)	✔(4)
Preeclampsia	✔(4)	✔(4)
Premature Labor	✔(4)	✔(4)
Prolapsed Cord	✔(4)	✔(4)
Pyelonephritis	✔(4)	✔(4)
RH Incompatability	✔(4)	✔(4)
Sickle Cell Disease	✔(4)	✔(4)
Stillbirth	✔(4)	✔(4)
Vaginal Birth after Cesarean Birth	✔(4)	✔(4)
Uterine Rupture	✔(4)	✔(4)
Monitoring		
General Anesthesia	✔(4)	✔(4)
Regional Anesthesia	✔(4)	✔(4)
Systemic Analgesia	✔(4)	✔(4)
Hemodynamics	✔(4)	✔(4)
Baseline	✔(4)	✔(4)
Cardiac Rhythms	✔(4)	✔(4)
Decelerations -- Early	✔(4)	✔(4)
Decelerations -- Late	✔(4)	✔(4)
Decelerations -- Prolonged	✔(4)	✔(4)
Decelerations -- Variable	✔(4)	✔(4)

Michelle Kimberly Neal, RN - Traveler   **Labor and Delivery**

Using the scale(s) below, please complete the following skill self assessment based upon your experience within the last 2 years.

Proficiency   [1] None [2] Intermittent [3] Experienced [4] Supervise/Teach

Frequency   [1] Never/Observed Only [2] Less than 6 times/year [3] Twice a Month [4] Daily - Weekly

Assessment/Patient Care Continued

	Proficiency 1 2 3 4	Frequency 1 2 3 4
Perinatal Vital Signs	✓(4)	✓(4)
Presence of Clonus	✓(4)	✓(4)
Variability	✓(4)	✓(4)
Post Partem		
General		
Apgar Scoring	✓(4)	✓(4)
Eye Prophylaxis	✓(4)	✓(4)
Initial Vital Signs	✓(4)	✓(4)
Newborn Scoring Scale	✓(4)	✓(4)
Post Partum		
Bladder Distention	✓(4)	✓(4)
Breast Feeding	✓(4)	✓(4)
DVT (Deep Vein Thrombosis)	✓(4)	✓(4)
Episiotomy	✓(4)	✓(4)
Fluid Balance	✓(4)	✓(4)
Fundal Height	✓(4)	✓(4)
Lochia Amount	✓(4)	✓(4)
Maternal Vital Signs	✓(4)	✓(4)
Lacerations	✓(4)	✓(4)
Maternal Hemorrhage	✓(4)	✓(4)
Retained Placenta	✓(4)	✓(4)

Medications/Therapeutic Interventions

	Proficiency 1 2 3 4	Frequency 1 2 3 4
Medications		
Administer IM/SC	✓(4)	✓(4)
Administer PO Medicaions	✓(4)	✓(4)
Anti-Tocolytics	✓(4)	✓(4)
Assist with Prostin Gel	✓(4)	✓(4)
Cervidil Insertion	✓(4)	✓(4)
Magnesium Sulfate	✓(4)	✓(4)
Oxytocin	✓(4)	✓(4)
Terbutaline	✓(4)	✓(4)
Tocolytics	✓(4)	✓(4)
Vitamin K	✓(4)	✓(4)
IV Therapy		
Fluid Challenge	✓(4)	✓(4)

Medications/Therapeutic Interventions Continued

	Proficiency 1 2 3 4	Frequency 1 2 3 4
Peripheral IV Insertion	✓(4)	✓(4)
Adverse Reactions	✓(4)	✓(4)
Assess/Maintain IV	✓(4)	✓(4)
Central Venous Catheter Care/Maintenance		
Fluid Resuscitation	✓(4)	✓(4)
Mix IV Infusion w/ Additives	✓(4)	✓(4)
Administer IV Meds	✓(4)	✓(4)
IV Drips	✓(4)	✓(4)
Pain Management		
Anesthesia Toxicity	✓(4)	✓(4)
Coaching Patient	✓(4)	✓(4)
Epidural Anesthesia/Analgesia	✓(4)	✓(4)
Epidural Block	✓(4)	✓(4)
Intrathecal Narcotics	✓(4)	✓(4)
Intravascular Injection	✓(4)	✓(4)
Moderate Sedation	✓(4)	✓(4)
Patient Controlled Analgesia	✓(4)	✓(4)
Positioning Patient	✓(4)	✓(4)
Signs/Symptoms of Dural Puncture	✓(4)	✓(4)
Spinal Anesthesia	✓(4)	✓(4)
Oxygen Administration		
Ambu-Bag	✓(4)	✓(4)
Isolette	✓(4)	✓(4)
Nasal Cannula and Face Mask	✓(4)	✓(4)
Portable Oxygen	✓(4)	✓(4)
Ventilation with Ambu Bag	✓(4)	✓(4)
Blood		
Administer Blood/Blood Products	✓(4)	✓(4)
Exchange Transfusions	✓(4)	✓(4)

Clinical COMPETENCY TESTING

Michelle Kimberly Neal, RN - Traveler

Labor and Delivery

Using the scale(s) below, please complete the following skill self assessment based upon your experience within the last 2 years.

Proficiency: (1) None (2) Intermittent (3) Experienced (4) Supervise/Teach

Frequency: (1) Never Observed Only (2) Less than 6 times/year (3) Twice a Month (4) Daily/Weekly

Procedures/Equipment	Proficiency 1 2 3 4	Frequency 1 2 3 4
General		
Catheter Insertion	4	4
Cesarean Section	4	4
Circulate for Cesarean Delivery	4	4
Circulate, Scrub for Bilateral Tubal Ligation	4	4
Conduct Contraction Stress Test	4	4
Conduct Non-Stress Test	4	4
Delivery Table Set-Up	3	3
Doppler	4	4
ECG Transducer (Phono or Abdominal)	4	4
Forceps Vaginal Delivery	4	4
Fundal Massage	3	3
Intrauterine Pressure Catheter	4	4
Perform Leopold's Maneuvers	3	3
Perform Sonogram	4	4
Positioning	4	4
Scrub for Cesarean Delivery	4	4
Set Up Cesarean Delivery	4	4
Spiral Electrode	4	4
Spontaneous Vaginal Delivery	4	4
Sterile Speculum Exam	4	4
Vacuum Extraction Delivery	4	4
Vaginal Exam	4	4
Urinary Catheterization -- Straight/Foley	4	4

Procedures/Equipment Continued	Proficiency 1 2 3 4	Frequency 1 2 3 4
Specimen Collection		
Arterial Line Draw	4	4
Butterfly Stick	4	4
Central Line Draw	4	4
Clean Catch Urine	4	4
Cultures-Blood	4	4
Dipstick Urine	4	4
Finger Stick	4	4
Stool	4	4
Sputum	4	4
Sterile Urine	4	4
Throat Swabs	4	4
Venipuncture	4	4
Cord Blood	4	4
Vaginal Cultures	4	4
Age Group Experience		
Age Groups		
0 - 30 Days	4	4
12 - 18 Years	4	4
18 - 39 Years	4	4
39 - 64 Years	4	4

CHAPTER 12

Healthcare Job Order Matching & Pitching Jobs: Coast 2 Coast Mentoring LLC.

Healthcare Job Order Matching & Pitching Jobs:

Important Scenarios and Planning Other Options:

At this point you should have an understanding about what your candidates' requirements are and what they are looking for. Based on that understanding you should have several options that are feasible to promote to candidate with confidence.

<u>Things to take note on:</u>

- – Most important trait in recruiting is to be transparent. Never lie being in healthcare recruiting that lie will eventually be exposed through time and you will lose candidates and rapport not to mention could damage your recruiting career. Best to be honest at all times. This builds trust, as we know trust goes a long way.

- Make sure that candidates understand full details such as pay packages, shift, hospital size and bed count of unit specialty, call-off policies, requested time off, block-scheduling etc.

- Always make sure you stay knowledgeable on what your competitors are offering to candidates. It's a punch in your gut hearing they have been submitted to a job order you have available as well.

At times candidate are indecisive and have no idea of what they want until you introduce that opportunity. Their needs are essential! Making their wants secondary. At least 70 percent of the time or greater, candidates are after higher pay rates. That being stated if you don't necessarily have a job order in the desired location requested, pitch a job that has crisis rate elsewhere. When it comes to money and if the pay is great enough, candidates are willing to consider. Doesn't hurt to pitch, worst they can say is no. Make sure your account manager are your best friends and who their preferred hospitals are. This strategy will give you another option to pitch to candidates. Advertise and promote your jobs or your competitors will.

Your commission relies on sealing a candidate an offer, providing job options molding the requirements the candidate has listed is your job. Make sure to advertise and promote exciting job opportunities that your agency has to offer, even it if it doesn't mold what candidate listed in requirements.

What Are at Stakes for Candidate Not Being Qualified:

Loss or rapport and trust can result in an unsuccessful job match between you and candidate. A lot of hours are spent building rapport with candidates and if they are not matched correctly, possibly could be a result of losing that candidate forever. Doesn't help with that words spreads instantly on social media networks such as Facebook, Instagram, LinkedIn to name a few. Negative comments and reviews can be headache to recover from.

Your agencies reputation can be tarnished if a candidate backs out last second or gets terminated. Note agencies promote and advertise quality and qualified candidate to hospitals, so when they are unable to back what they stated they would cater causes everyone to look bad. This could cause hospital to consider other agencies candidate over your company when the next job order develops. If it happens multiple times, the hospital could possibly not use services in future. Thousands of dollars are spent to onboard a candidate. Costs associated with drug test, backgrounds, medical records, onboarding and orientation costs not to mention others.

More than losing money, it's your responsibility to provide the most qualified candidates on behalf of the patient, family members and hospital your representing. Sending unqualified candidates can result in a life being lost!

Questions Candidates Should Ask During Interviews to Prospective Hospitals:

- Is block or self-scheduling allowed?
- What color scrubs are required? Are they provided?

- What EMR system does your hospital use?
- Is On-call required? What are your on-call requirements?
- What are the details of orientation?
- Do you extend candidates often?
- What is your hospital average patient ratios?
- What is the unit bed count?
- Is floating required? If so, are travelers first to float?
- Are weekends required?
- How would you describe the atmosphere of the unit?
- How are your experiences typically with travelers?

Make sure the candidate asks questions that are important to them being they are work on that unit.

Healthcare Recruiter Profile Submission Packet Checklist:
(For recruiters to cover with healthcare candidates before submitting to hospital)

- Detail all aspects of pay package such as hourly rate, how much per hour is taxed versus nontaxed, housing stipend or housing, overtime, on-call pay
- Best times available to be interviewed and schedule availability
- Time requested off possibly by candidate
- Verify if candidate is comfortable floating or not
- Know what shift candidate is willing to work – Nights, Days or MIDS

- Make sure all details of contract are laid out on the table and candidate acknowledges and understands fully
- Go over on-call policies
- Discuss medical benefits as well as travel reimbursement
- Go over all guidelines and requirements
- Discuss all orientation details

This information should be technically on profile cover sheet.

CHAPTER 13
Understanding Healthcare Pay Packages: Coast 2 Coast Mentoring LLC.

Understanding Healthcare Pay Packages:

Healthcare Travel Pay Packages:

Pay usually has four major divisions: hourly taxable wages, untaxed meals and incidentals, housing and travel. How much your agency pays a candidate depends on bill rates and what cut your agency takes. Bill rates vary from hospital to hospital as well as agencies at the same hospital.

Compare your pay to full pizza. The hospital pays your agency with a full pizza, and your company divides that up to where the agency makes money but keeps the candidate happy by providing a pay package that is competitive with the market. In below sections will describe in detail, pay package breakdowns for candidates.

The per diem program is a huge benefit to travelers and why they consider traveling over permanent staff. General Services Administration (GSA) establishes the per diem rates for the lower 48 Continental United States (CONUS), which are the maximum allowances that federal employees are reimbursed for expenses incurred while on official travel. The CONUS per diem rate for an area is actually three allowances: the lodging allowance, the meals allowance and the incidental expense allowance. Most of the CONUS (approximately 2600 counties) are covered by the standard CONUS per diem rate of $151 ($96 lodging, $55 meals and incidental expenses). In fiscal year (FY) 2020, there are 322 Non-Standard Areas (NSAs) that have per diem rates higher than the standard CONUS rate. Since FY 2005, NSA rates have been based on Average Daily Rate (ADR) data from the lodging industry, which GSA obtains through a contract with a leading provider of lodging industry data. For more about how per diem rates are determined, visit Factors Influencing Lodging Rates. The ADR is a widely accepted lodging-industry measure based upon a property's room rental revenue divided by the number of rooms rented as reported by the hotel property to the contractor. This calculation provides GSA with the average rate in a given area. To sum up, the program states some expenses are tax deductible and others are nontaxed reimbursements. Reimbursements are often referred to as per diems, meal and incidentals and housing stipends. Agencies are reminded that the Federal Travel Regulation allows for actual expense reimbursement when per diem rates are insufficient to meet necessary expenses

The General Services Administration (GSA) establishes travel policy (includes per diem) only for federal employees (excluding federal contractors) on official travel away from their local duty station or areas defined by their agency, and cannot speak for any other state, city, or agency's travel policy. To qualify for non-taxed reimbursements according to the IRS, the traveler must maintain a tax home usually fifty miles or greater from the location of assignment. The Revenue Ruling 73-529—also outlined in the 2015 IRS Publication 463—outlines three factors to determine a tax home, as they apply to the traveler. You must check off two of the three factors below to consider this your tax home.

- **You perform part of your business in the area of your main home and use that home for lodging while doing business. For example, you are a travel nurse, but are still on per diem with your original hospital and often work there when going home between assignments.**
- **You have living expenses at your main home that you duplicate because your business requires you to be away from home. For example, you are paying rent or a mortgage in your home city but also paying rent while on travel contract.**
- **You have not abandoned the area where your main home is located. You have family members living there, or you often visit and use that home for lodging. You also keep up with your community contacts in that area with friends and family. For example, between assignments you go home and stay at your tax home. You visit with family and friends and keep in touch with them while on contract.**

Travelers are encouraged to return to tax home once per year. Smart travelers maintain registry or per diem locally in their tax home. This ensures work in-between assignments. Never hurts to have steady work especially when providing for a family.

You are not a tax official or representative so do not act like one. Explain the details in depth to your candidates so there are no bumps in the road. From that point it's the candidate's responsibility to evaluate and deem whether its feasible to move forward. If they continue to have tax questions, advise them to speak with an accountant they trust.

Non-Taxable Travel Nurse Pay

The most alluring advertisement travel nursing agencies use to get candidates in the door is the infamous "tax advantage plan". This can also be referred to as per-diem, stipends, reimbursements or a combination of all three. What this basically means is that if your candidate is traveling away from your home for work, there are certain expenses that are tax deductible and certain reimbursements that are non-taxable. The most common types of stipends or reimbursements that you will hear about in the travel nursing world are referred to as meals and incidentals (incidentals include taxi/bus fares, parking, and tips), lodging or housing stipends, and travel reimbursements which cover your expenses to and from each assignment; other non-taxable items can include retirement plans, license reimbursements and health insurance. When travel nursing companies advertise pay rates, they will often tell you a blended rate. A blended rate combines an hourly taxable wage such as $20 an hour with your non-taxable reimbursements and stipends to give you a higher hourly rate. Here is an example of a typical pay package: $20 per hour – taxable base rate that is reported to the IRS $250 per week for meals and incidentals – non-taxable $2,000 a month for lodging – non-taxable $500 for travel reimbursement – non-taxable Candidates blended rate is calculated by breaking down your non-taxable stipends into an hourly rate and adding it to their taxable base rate.

For instance, if candidate worked 36 hours per week on a 13-week assignment, their hourly rate would look something like this based on the above scenario:

$250/wk. for meals X 13 weeks: $3,250
$2,000 per month lodging X 3 months: $6,000
$500 travel reimbursement (one time): $500

Total: $9,750
Divided by total hours worked/468 hours
Non-taxable stipend pay per hour: = $20.83
Add base pay: +$20
Total blended rate: $40.83 per hour

Flex Pay and Rigid Pay:

There are two different types of pay packages: flex pay and rigid pay. Flex pay packages allow to mix and match, add or subtract various non-taxable stipends such as healthcare, retirement, and license reimbursements to your pay package, while rigid pay packages are non-negotiable. The benefit of flex pay is that candidate can decrease their hourly taxable base rate and increase their non-taxable earnings by adding more benefits such as 401K. Many travel agencies have to be careful not to enter the illegal realm of wage re-characterization when dealing with flex pay packages. To learn more about wage re-characterization visit traveltax.com.

Travel Nurse Overtime:

There are some travel contracts offering overtime; for example, some agencies will ask candidate if they want to work 4 days a week instead of 3 days a week. Overtime by law has to be paid time and a half of your taxable base rate. So, if candidate makes $20 and hour, then your overtime pay will be $30 an hour. In the world of nursing, $30 an hour isn't really that much extra money for an extra shift; however, over the long run it does add up. If this is something candidate is considering doing than make sure candidates negotiate a higher taxable rate for lower non-taxable stipends if possible so that they really get more bang for their buck.

Disadvantages of Non-taxable Stipend Pay Travel Nursing Pay package:

The allure of low taxable income and high non-taxable income sounds appealing, but there are some potential downsides to this scenario. The first disadvantage comes into play when candidate is attempting to get a loan. Most banks do not take into consideration stipends and reimbursements when it comes to giving out money, so if candidate is trying to qualify for a loan, it looks like candidate only earned $30,000 in one year instead of $60,000. Also have to take into consideration retirement. I know many candidates aren't necessarily thinking about their social security check right now, but it is important to take into consideration that the social security payments are based on 35 of candidate's highest income earning years. Non-taxable money is not considered income. Last but not least, if candidates get injured on the job, candidates they receive 2/3 of hourly taxable base rate.

Travel Nursing Pay: Things to Consider:

With all things considered, travelers pay rate, is very comparable to a staff nurse's pay rate. However, there are some out of pocket expenses travel nurses have to be aware of that regular staff nurses don't have to consider; Most travel nursing agencies do not offer paid time off. If candidates are thinking of taking a vacation or are taking time off in between assignments, then they will not be paid. Most travelers have to pay for their own certifications such as BLS and ACLS Sometimes travel nursing agencies will not pay for candidates annual physical and TB tests If a candidate wants to take an assignment that is across the country, travel reimbursement might not cover the entire cost. It is important to express to your candidate to budget and prepare for the unknown. Make sure your candidates are prepared and organized.

Tips to Make Traveling a Pleasant Experience:

All of this talk about taxes and the IRS can be a little scary. Here are a few easy tips to follow to make candidates experience a little less complicated:

- Tell candidate to maintain a mileage log. Candidate will have to write down their odometer reading the beginning of the year on January 1 and again at the end of the year on Dec 31. If candidate starts traveling in the middle of the year, they can look back at their maintenance records for previous odometer readings. They must also document their mileage to and from candidates place of employment.
- Return to candidate's tax home in between assignments if possible or at a minimum of once per year. Candidate needs to document when they travel back to candidate's tax home.
- Tell candidate to try to maintain a PRN or agency job in the same vicinity as their tax home. The IRS would like to know that you do business on a regular basis where they live.
- There is no need to keep track of meal or grocery receipts. The IRS gives candidates a set stipend for meals. If candidate exceeds the stipend they are considered to be living above their means and will not be reimbursed.
- Tell candidate to keep a copy of all of their travel contracts. Make sure candidates have a beginning and ending date on them. This proves that they were really working on a temporary basis.
- Tell candidate don't work in a city more than 12 months in a

24-month period. The IRS will think they abandoned their tax home.

- There are tax people who specialize specifically in travel nursing. I recommend getting in contact with these people prior to starting their assignment. If they want to tackle this on their own, then I recommend getting organized.

Don't let the IRS or financial aspects of travel nursing scare your candidates. Travel nursing should be an enjoyable experience not an accounting nightmare. As with any tax issues, candidates should seek advice from a licensed tax professional before filing. This only offers suggestions and isn't meant to be tax advice. We leave that to the pros. Professionals can help you through this experience in combination with educating candidates about nursing pay packages. It sounds complicated in the beginning, but the more you learn the lingo, the more prepared you will be to negotiate your candidates next travel contract.

Hourly Wage:

Every pay package must include a taxable hourly wage. While the IRS doesn't set a specific "minimum wage" for travelers, it should be in the best practice of your company to create a fair market value for your travelers. For most agencies this would include $15 to $18/ hour for allied health or non-specialty positions and $20 to $22/hour for specialty positions. It is not advisable to go under these wages as the IRS considers it to be wage recharacterization, and if audited, the company and its travelers could be held to some stiff penalties. Some agencies start at a $25 to $30/hour minimum. A recommended guideline for this is to make sure that travelers in a similar specialty or assigned to the same facility are paid a consistent hourly wage.

Housing:

Housing can be broken down in two ways. Either the company is providing housing, or the traveler is taking the housing stipend. It is more beneficial for the traveler to take the housing stipend for two primary reasons. First, they will have a choice in where they stay. Everyone's definition of comfortable and acceptable are different. Why risk an unhappy traveler? Remember, once that lease is signed, you can't break it. Most travelers get to their location a few days in advance, and this arrangement would give them time to check out some options before signing a lease agreement, especially with today's online search engines for housing. Most locations should have multiple options for your traveler. The second reason the housing stipend is more beneficial for them is because it can be given as a nontaxable amount. If the housing stipend in Gallup, New Mexico is $2,200/month, but housing only costs $2,000, then with the stipend the traveler has an extra $200/month. If the company provides housing, they would need to take that extra $200 and put it into the hourly taxable rate or pay it as a bonus, which is taxed at a high rate. You can never pay for housing and pay a housing stipend as well. This is considered "double dipping."

Meals & Incidentals:

M&IE guidelines are similar to housing stipends in that they are set by the IRS. By visiting www.gsa.gov, you can determine the set per diem standards for cities and states across the country. Per diems may also be referred to as meals and incidental stipends. Let's say that the daily M & IE (meals and incidental expenses) is $51/day. This breaks down to $357/week. Thus, the maximum amount you could pay for per diem in this area is $357/week. Again, this is the maximum amount for that area. The hospital bill rates will likely restrict a rate this high. You'll more likely be looking at $150 to $300/week for the contract. It is important to note that travelers must always receive M&IE. They can never just receive the housing allowance.

Travel:

Many recruiters may not even offer travel and instead put that money into the per diems or housing for their traveler, so they are receiving the benefits over the entire contract, not just at the very beginning or end of the contract. While a travel stipend can be used to cover the cost of a flight for the traveler, it is more often than not used to subsidize the traveler's expenses to and from an assignment. The current IRS mileage rates are set at 54 cents per mile. You can pay your traveler up to that amount. Some companies recommend sticking with a flat rate, so in this circumstance you might offer a $200 travel stipend on the first paycheck and $200 on the last. Refer to your company's mileage reimbursement policy to confirm the amount to pay for travel.

Overall Review of Pay Packages:

As stated previously you are not a tax representative so always remind yourself. You are not a psychic and have no clue what they claim on W-2s. They can possibly have wage garnishments or contributing to a 401k retirement plan. Always state "estimated "when quoting pay take home after taxes.

It's okay if you are overwhelmed with information at this point. That's normal. Understand the more you practice composing pay packages the faster you will become at ease and comfortable. Find open jobs orders you are looking to promote and manufacture a few packages until you feel comfortable.

Understand the Healthcare Market:

Now that you gained an understanding for pay packages a little, know that every company package pays differently. When it comes to competing with another agency for a candidate that both agencies have the same hospital, it's important to investigate how the other agency is packaging their pay package to candidate.

The difference between pitching a package with gross versus net take home is around $150 to $200 difference in pay.

Some agencies promote in terms of hourly pay. They may promote $80 an hour to allure the candidate, but after taking out agency overhead and insurance the candidate might possibly be taking home less than the pay you are sponsoring.

When competing with another agency to place the same candidate, have the candidate send your competitors contract so you are able to compare. Transparency at this point is best, being they will appreciate your integrity and hard work. Most agencies or recruiters do not take the time to hold their candidates' hand throughout the process.

Pay Considerations:

Pay consideration includes overtime rates, travel reimbursement, cancelation policies, missed shift policies, holiday pay rates, call back rate and on-call. When quoting healthcare pay packages ensure everything mentioned is taken into account.

Some hospital at times offer crucial, elevated or crisis rates when a job order is difficult to fill. This will allure candidates to become interested, therefore filling the job order quickly. Travelers get excited when those rates are rolled out and expect increased production.

CHAPTER 14

Negotiating with Hospitals: Coast 2 Coast Mentoring LLC.

Negotiating Rates and Contracts:

Once you have gained rapport with your hospital by providing qualified travelers who complete assignments with no issues, it's easier to negotiate rates and contract requirements. No point to negotiate unless you or your agency have proven value. Here are some great negotiating tips.

- Coach the hospital on elements such as competitors' rates, housing costs and other determining factors
- Know what their problems are and show them through examples how to solve the problem to create value and separate yourself apart.
- Form a pay tier that differentiates regular pay and crisis rate for positions they are having issues filling
- Negotiate a bill rate where you are able to fill the position rather then state a bill rate you feel they want to hear
- Discuss with hospital about forty-eight-hour guarantees, Block

and self-scheduling, or twenty-six-week contracts to make the position more desirable in order to help fill in a timely manner

Handling Rocky Conversations:

Rocky conversation will occur. How you handle these situations will display professionalism which will earn respect with travelers. Never avoid tough conversations. These conversations if handled correctly, will build trust and rapport with your hospitals. Educate the hospital on how vital communication is and providing full job descriptions in order to help fill their job orders at a rapid pace.

Job details are crucial in finding the most suitable candidates for a successful match

Communication is important. Educate the hospital that if they do not act fast by not returning calls or emails, they will lose a phenomenal candidate. It takes recruiters time and hard work to retrieve these candidates. Clarify to hospital that no responses can gear recruiters from send great candidates their way. Investigate why hospital isn't responding and offer your assistance. Ask if they are overloaded? If so, how may you assist and relieve some pressure?

Termination is always a touchy subject and hard to deal with mentality. It's important to move forward immediately and be available for your hospital during that time. Find out why candidate was terminated. Was it for not showing up, clinical errors or attitude? If the issue is coachable, this gives an opportunity for you and your agency to contact candidate to create a solution that will impact a better experience for the hospital without canceling the contract. There are two-sides to a story as we all know.

CHAPTER 15

Closing Your Candidate: Coast 2 Coast Mentoring LLC.

Closing Your Candidate with Offer Pending:

Time to celebrate, you have an offer granted by hospital. What are the nest steps you are probably wondering?

Let hope you impressed the hospital by providing a candidate molding their requirements in a timely manner.

Make sure to review the terms of contract, verify pay package is aligned with what was advertised by you. Candidate needs to be aware of hospital expectations and understand what is expected. If candidate has questions that have popped up last minute, address immediately.

Creating value and separating yourself from others is developed through time. It's a marathon, not a sprint! Catering your candidate at all times is necessary to keep them loyal and happy. Word of mouth is the best referral. If you don't cater to their needs another recruiter will.

It's important to go over what expected of your candidate. Check candidate's availability and create a timeline for compliance to be completed. If nurse has any doubts they need to be addressed on the spot.

Candidates at times get cold feet and hesitate to tell you. It's your duty to educate on the recruiting cycle and what to expect upcoming so they do not encounter bumps or hiccups. Constantly reassure candidate you are available to help and answer any questions.

Confirm candidate is ware by verbally accepting an offer for an assignment, the hospital and agency begin the process for compliance, scheduling and orientation. If they have any doubts about receiving an offer you need to investigate why and find a solution.

If you followed every step correctly to this point, the deal should have been closed well before this process. This is one of the easier steps in the recruiting cycle.

Handling Uncomfortable Conversations with Candidates:

Awkward and tough conversations are going to arise, it is the nature of the beast. Never let it frustrate to the point it ruins your workday and stops production. Deal with any issues immediately, builds a great travel experience for candidate. These issues do not disappear so it's best to deal with them heads on. Be polite and respectful at all times. Do not address the person, tackle the issue.

In regard to terminations, investigates the causes to why candidate was terminated. Find out if they are clinical issues that could possibly be coachable. If its non-clinical, like nurse being rude and having an attitude, pull candidate aside in a respectable manner and educate them that it cannot continue. People need to vent at times, so lend an ear at those times. Don't be too empathetic and allow them to justify and explain their behavior. Always trust your instincts. If candidates are causing issues and you feel is not a fit, no shame in releasing that candidate.

CHAPTER 16

Hospital Onboarding and Traveling Experience: Coast 2 Coast Mentoring LLC.

Hospital Onboarding:

Onboarding teaches New Hires about their roles in the hospital. Proper onboarding procedures include training for employees. Training provides candidates with the knowledge they need to excel in their job role. By aligning new employees with their role, they feel needed and important in the hospital. Once the candidate has signed the contract, the onboarding process begins. Compliance is not the only element to onboarding which will be discussed, there are other aspects.

Onboarding helps candidates understand what is expected, the overall expectations of agency and the requirements for them to have a positive experience. The groundwork has already been established for a successful partnership. Now it's time to display your value. Make sure to always keep an open line of communication as it vital to candidates completing a successful contract. Train your candidate through your company processes. Last thing you want is to lose candidate over a minor error, especially working to get to this point.

Educate your candidate. Set expectations on credentialing requirements, orientation, payroll, timesheet process, housing, emergency contacts, and any other hospital and assignment information.

Examples of Credentialing Requirements:

- **Physical:** Within the past twelve months. A physical is a statement from a doctor that verifies the employee is able to work and can perform the functions of the job.
- **Hepatitis B:** Hep B Titer OR three vaccine series OR Decline.
- **Varicella:** Titer or vaccine. Varicella is chickenpox. These vaccinations are good forever. **MMR (Measles/Mumps/Rubella):** Titers or two vaccine series. A titer is a blood test that gets sent to the lab to check immunity. These are good forever unless otherwise specified by the hospital.
- **TB (PPD):** Annual. The Tuberculosis test is an injection into the arm and the date and time is logged. The RN must return to the place where it was placed or an ER between forty-eight and seventy-two hours. If it is read before forty-eight hours, it is invalid; and if it is read after seventy-two hours, it is invalid. Some hospitals will require a two-step TB in which a TB is placed and a second one is placed after two weeks of the first one being read. If there is proof of a positive TB, then a chest X-ray is required and must be done every two years.
- **Flu:** Annual. The flu shot is usually only required during the winter months. Some may decline for medical (allergic) or religious reasons. A hospital may cancel a contract if the traveler refuses the flu shot, or they may require the traveler to wear a mask.

- **Certifications:** Front and back copies of all certifications, BLS, ACLS, etc.
- **State licenses:** Front and back copies of all state nursing licenses.
- **Driver's license:** Copy of current, active driver's license
- **Social Security Card or Passport:** Copy of social security card or current passport

Customer Experience:

Customer experience is of critical importance to the sustained growth of a business. It's important to ensure a positive customer experience so customers build brand loyalty and affinity, evangelize your service and refer their friends, and leave you positive customer reviews that will help your business retain revenue and earn new customers. Customer experience is the interaction between you and your agency and hospitals and candidates. The customer experience generates loyalty.

If a candidates and hospitals receive proper customer experience, they will most likely be loyal to you for years to come. Your skills as a recruiter could determine whether you receive referrals or not. Referrals are the strongest leads in the healthcare recruiting industry. As an account manager, the experience you provide to your hospitals will earn you a slot on their preferred providers list. The happier the hospital is, the greater of a chance you will be first to be call once the next job order develops. Meaning your candidates profile will be reviewed first increasing the percentages of sealing an offer.

Managing the complete recruitment journey from start to finish is the definition of customer experience. It's consistent. Meaning always be there for your candidate. Recruiter and agencies who can perfect this process for their candidate will develop higher retention rates, loyalty and referrals.

Ideas to Create a Stronger Customer Experience:

- Create a clear customer experience vision
- Understand who your candidates are
- Create an emotional connection with your candidates
- Capture candidate feedback in real time
- Use a quality framework for development of your team
- Act upon regular employee feedback
- Do want you state you're going to do in the timeline you outlined
- Send notes or gifts on birthdays to show appreciation
- Invest interest in their hobbies and passions
- Never give off the impression your too busy
- Be engaged in conversations
- Be a great listener
- Plan weekly calls, texts or emails

CHAPTER 17

Bonus: Coast 2 Coast Mentoring LLC.

BONUS: Facebook Groups to Join that Will Boast Production a Minimum 25% if Used Every day: Coast 2 Coast Mentoring LLC.

- **Travel Nurses: The $1800+ Gross/Week, $50+/Hour, Travel Nursing Job Board.**
- **Travel Nurse – Odyssey Nurse**
- **RN & LPN-Travel Nurse Positions**
- **Travel Nurse Urgent Jobs- USSI**
- **Travel Nursing: The Premium Job Board**
- **Travel RN Job Group**
- **Travel Nurse Network**
- **ICU Travel Nursing jobs**
- **Travel RN/LPN/CNA & Recruiters**
- **ICU Travel RN Nursing Jobs**
- **Local per-diem and contract nursing jobs nationwide**
- **Gypsy Soul Prime Travel Assignments Job Board**
- **Travel RN Jobs Travel Nursing Opportunities-California**

- **Travel Nurses: The $1900+ Gross/Week, Travel Nursing Job Board**
- **Telemetry PCU Stepdown RN Travel Nurse Jobs**
- **Labor Delivery RN Travel Nursing Jobs**
- **L&D Job Board UNCENSORED**
- **Southern California Nurse Job Opportunities**
- **PACU Travel Jobs Board**
- **Labor and Delivery Travel Nurse Jobs making 2k plus a week, Great locations**
- **California Nurse Job Opportunities**
- **CNA & LPN Travel Jobs**
- **Arizona Travel Jobs**
- **Midwest Travel Nurses**
- **California Travel Nurses Network**
- **Premium Travel Nursing Jobs**
- **ER Nursing Travel Jobs!**
- **Travel Nurse R Us**
- **Travel Nursing Jobs**
- **RV Travel Nurse Adventures**
- **New Travel Nursing Jobs: Coast to Coast**
- **Healthcare Gypsy**
- **Staffing the country, one hospital at a time!**
- **The Travel Nursing Jobs Connection: Your Link to Jobs & Recruiters**
- **Travel Nursing: MedSurg/Tele/Stepdown Travel Nurse Job Board**
- **ER Travel Nurses**
- **Scrub Squad 1978 The $2200+ Gross/Week, Travel Nursing Job Board**

- Travel Nursing
- CNA TRAVEL ASSIGNMENTS – JOB BOARD
- Travel Nurse Jobs
- North Carolina Travel Nurse Jobs
- OR RN TRAVEL JOBS
- Registered nurse
- Med/Surg Nursing Travel & Permanent Jobs
- South Carolina Travel Nurse Jobs
- Employment Psychiatric Travel Nurse
- NICU Travel Nursing Jobs
- CNA & LPN Travel Jobs—NonSponsored
- Travel Nursing: California
- OR Travel Jobs
- Travel Nursing: Choice Job Connections
- California Travel RN's: JOBS & OPPORTUNITIES
- Meet Vetted Travel Nurses actively seeking jobs!!!
- Travel and Perm (Operating Room) Nurse Jobs
- Psychiatry RN Travel Nurse Jobs
- Travel Nursing:Assignments Wanted
- Not Your Average: Travel Nurse Job Board
- South Texas Nurse Job Opportunities
- Respiratory Therapy and Nursing Travelers
- Colorado Travel Nurse Jobs
- ER Nurse Premium Pay Travel Jobs
- ICU Travel Nursing Jobs!
- Travel Nurse Jobs and Referrals
- Oregon Travel Nurse Jobs
- LPN & LVN Travel & Local Jobs
- Arizona Travel Nursing

- **Premium NICU Travel Assignments**
- **Nursing Jobs in United States**
- **ICU**
- **CNA JOB'S NATION WIDE TRAVEL AND LOCAL**
- **HAWAII TRAVEL NURSES – OAHU – MAUI – KAUAI – BIG ISLAND**
- **The Texas Nurse Traveler**
- **Alaska Travel Nurse Jobs**
- **Massachusetts Travel Nurse Jobs**
- **Travel Nurse Jobs – (ENLC) Compact States**
- **CNA & LPN Jobs**
- **Home Health Travel RN Group**
- **LPN Travel Assignments**
- **Travel RN Jobs & Housing: The Carolinas (NC/SC)**
- **CNA/LPN Premium Pay Travel Assignments Group**
- **RRT: Registered Respiratory Therapist Travel Jobs**
- **North Texas Nurse Job Opportunities**
- **Adventures of Travel/Perm Nurses and Healthcare Professionals in Colorado**
- **CNA & CMA Local & Travel Job**
- **Hawaii Travel Nurse Jobs**
- **Tennessee Travel Nurse Jobs**
- **Travel Nurse Jobs – Indiana, Crossroads of America**
- **Rural Travel Nursing Group**
- **Florida Nurse Job Opportunities**
- **Nurse Jobs Kansas City**
- **Missouri Travel Nurse Jobs**
- **Travel Nurses Take Indiana**
- **Peds Traveling RNS**

- **TRAVEL (OR) TECH JOBS**
- **Traveling nursing in Nebraska Job's Board**
- **Travel Cath Lab, IR, and EP Nurse and Tech Jobs**
- **Travel Nurse RN Jobs Kentucky/Ohio/West Virginia/ Tennessee**
- **Florida Travel Allied and Nursing jobs**
- **North Carolina Travel Nurse RN Jobs**
- **Travel Nursing – OKLAHOMA**
- **Alaska Travel Nurse RN jobs**
- **Travel Nursing – North vs South**
- **Texas Travel Nursing and Allied Healthcare jobs**
- **Correctional Travel Nurses**
- **Travel Allied Health Job Board**
- **Travel Nurse – Arizona**
- **Long Term Care/Skilled Nursing Travel Group**
- **Florida Travel Nursing and Therapy Jobs**
- **Washington Travel Nurse Network**
- **Nevada Travel Nurse Network**
- **Illinois Nurse Job Opportunities**
- **Skilled Nursing Long Term Care RN Travel Jobs**
- **Per Diem Nursing In California**
- **PACU Travel Nursing Jobs**
- **Travel Nurses Take Texas**
- **Oregon Travel Nurse Network**
- **Central California Nurse Job Opportunities**
- **Texas Travel Nurse Jobs**
- **Illinois RN Jobs**
- **Arizona Travel Nurse Jobs**
- **Travel Nurse Job Board- Washington & Oregon**

- **South Carolina Travel Nurse RN Jobs**
- **Travel Cath Lab Travel Jobs**
- **RN & LPN Case Management**
- **Travel Nursing Jobs: East Coast**
- Kentucky Travel Nurse Jobs
- Physical Therapy Jobs (USA Only)
- Medical Assistant Jobs (USA Only)
- Hospice travel nurses
- RV Travel Nurses
- Travel Nursing In The Midwest
- Washington Travel Nurse Jobs
- Seattle Travel Nursing Jobs
- Travel Nurse Jobs: Non-Compact States
- Georgia Travel Nurse RN Jobs
- Pediatric Job board (all jobs peds) PICU, CV, ED, Peds, Pedi OR,
- Atlanta Travel Nursing Job
- Tennessee Nurse Job Opportunities
- Arizona Nurse Job Opportunities
- Travel Nurses-Dallas/Ft. Worth
- Dialysis Travel Nurses and Techs
- Travel Nurses Take North & South Carolina
- EAST COAST JOBS
- TRAVELING CASE MANAGERS AND TRAVELING SOCIAL WORKERS
- Register Nurse & Health Care Jobs USA
- Nurse Yuko's ECC Adventure
- New York Nurse Job Opportunities
- Travel Nurses Take Louisiana
- Traveling Nurses & Surgical Tech Housing

- Travel Nursing 101
- Registered Nurses

Definitions of Basic Medical Terms: Coast 2 Coast Mentoring LLC.

Definitions of Basic Medical Terms:

Anatomy: Parts of the body and its general structure.

Gynecology: Study and treatment of the female urinary tract and reproductive organs.

Hematology: Treatment of blood diseases and malignancies.

Microbiology: Related to bacterial and viral infections.

Neonatal: Special care for newborn babies with high dependency needs.

Neurology: Related to the disorders of the brain, spinal cord, or general nervous system.

Oncology: Chemotherapy treatments for cancer.

Pathology: The names for disorders and diseases.

Pediatrics: Medical assistance of infants.

Psychiatry: The study and treatment of mental disorders.

Rheumatology: Related to musculoskeletal disorders (bones, joints, muscles, etc.).

Surgery: Physical operative procedures.

Urology: Related to problems with the bladder and kidneys.

Here are some common descriptive words when talking about patients and circumstance:

Abatement: A reduction in severity of symptoms.

Abiotic: Not related to living organisms.

Abortive: Cutting short the course of a disease.

Abrasion: Friction wearing away of the top layer of skin.

Abruption: A sudden breaking away or breaking off.

Accessory: Extra or supplementary to the main element.

Ambulatory: Ability to walk.

Analgesia: Loss of pain where pain would normally be evident without loss of consciousness.

Benign: An abnormal growth that is not life-threatening.

Cavity: Hollow space in the body containing one organ or more.

Compression: To apply pressure to stop bleeding or prevent further injury.

Etiology: The cause of a certain condition.

Exacerbation: Deterioration of a condition.

Hematemesis: Blood in vomit.

Iatrogenic: A condition that appears as a result of treatment of another condition.

Idiopathic: Of unknown cause.

Intractable: Difficult to cure or alleviate.

Referred pain: Pain that is felt in another area to the original source of this pain.

Reflux: Going in a backward direction.

Remission: Disappearance of signs of disease.

Stimulus: Elicits a physiological response.

Subcutaneous: Just beneath the skin

Syndrome: A set of symptoms that indicate towards a certain condition, disease or abnormality.

CHAPTER 18

Company & Personal History: Coast 2 Coast Mentoring LLC.

About Coast 2 Coast Mentoring LLC.

Coast 2 Coast Mentoring LLC., founded and owned by Noah Neumiller, is a unique coaching program on the healthcare recruiting market today available to those who are motivated to succeed in this industry. My mission is to provide a foundation and enlighten you on the A-Z's of healthcare recruiting. This manual will utilize 17 years' recruiting experience to develop your strengths and to utilize them to improve quality, maximize performance, increase profitability, and promote accountability as well as sustained growth.

Coast 2 Coast Mentoring LLC. believes in helping others through empathy, passion and promoting equality and opportunity for all. Most importantly we believe in saving lives through a commitment to our partnerships with hospitals and healthcare medical centers across the country in providing the most qualified nurses and allied health professionals as well as the duty to those travelers to ensure to our best abilities that they have supportive and encouraging travel experiences.

Short Bio: Coast 2 Coast Mentoring LLC.

Short Biography:

Noah Neumiller
Director of Lead Healthstaff in Tarzana, CA

Growing up in West Hollywood, the youngest of three brothers. My father, an owner of a very successful plumbing business, while my mother was a stay at home Jewish wife.

My parents divorced early on. I was too young to know what was going on, just that my mom wasn't home anymore. I was led to believe that my mom abandoned my brothers and I. My grandparents, aunt and uncle always said she left us, but they never told me of all the abuse toward her that led up to the divorce ultimately leaving me lost and confused. I was never told that my father was addicted to drugs and alcohol until he went to rehab, which took a mental toll on me at an early age that led me down the wrong path.

In high school I began to party, where I was introduced to marijuana and cocaine, developing an addiction that plagued me for years. The awaking for me came in January of 2003, when my best friend Nick Eckland struck a tree while under the influence of alcohol and was killed along with three other passengers in the vehicle. I mourned for months before pulling myself together, as he was like a brother to me. It wasn't easy, but I needed to change my life and end the drug and alcohol abuse.

In 2004, I graduated from Fresno City College with an associate degree in business administration alongside a 3.6 G.P.A. Shortly after, I was recruited off LinkedIn to become a Jr. Recruiter at ReadyLink Healthcare, where I set an unprecedented production record, earning praise from both industry leaders and hospitals.

That being said, I have learned quite a few things about healthcare staffing with my 17 years of experience. After being designated a Placement Manager in 2013, I rose to Director, overseeing the travel placement of healthcare professionals in the industry and staying consistently seated as the top producer, amassing more than $8 million in career billings. Despite my stellar numbers, I continue to be inspired by the relationships I have built and lives I affect every day. My ultimate goal is to provide superior service for my clients and candidates, so that they in return can deliver superior healthcare to patients.

■ ■ ■

Noah Neumiller – Director of Recruitment
Lead Healthstaff
18425 Burbank Blvd., Suite 508, Tarzana, CA 91356
877.247.8847 Toll-free | 714.287.5251 Direct
877.747.9338 Efax | 714.287.5251 Texting
Travel@leadhealthstaff.com | www.leadhealthstaff.com

Printed in Great Britain
by Amazon